On
Film

STEPHEN MULHALL

On
Film

London and New York

First published 2002
by Routledge
11 New Fetter Lane, London EC4P 4EE

Simultaneously published in the USA and Canada
by Routledge
29 West 35th Street, New York, NY 10001

Routledge is an imprint of the Taylor & Francis Group

Typeset in Joanna and DIN by Keystroke, Jacaranda Lodge, Wolverhampton
Printed and bound in Great Britain by Biddles Ltd, Guildford and King's Lynn

British Library Cataloguing in Publication Data
A catalogue record for this book is available from the British Library

Library of Congress Cataloging in Publication Data
Mulhall, Stephen, 1962–
     On film / Stephen Mulhall.
        p. cm. – (Thinking in action)
     Includes bibliographical references (p.) and index.
     Contents: Kane's son, Cain's daughter : Ridley Scott's Alien – Making babies :
James Cameron's Aliens – Mourning sickness : David Fincher's Aliens 3 – The
monster's mother : Jean-Pierre Jeunet's Alien resurrection.
     1. Alien (Motion picture) 2. Science fiction films–History and criticism. I. Title.
II. Series

PN1997.A32253 M85 2001
791.43′72–dc21   2001038713

ISBN 0–415–24795–0 (hbk)
ISBN 0–415–24796–9 (pbk)

For
Eleanor

Few films produced over the last two decades have simultaneously achieved as much popular and critical success as the
four members of the 'Alien' series (*Alien* [1979]; *Aliens* [1986];
Alien^3 [1992]; *Alien Resurrection* [1997]). They focus on Flight
Lieutenant Ellen Ripley (played by Sigourney Weaver) as she
confronts the threat posed to herself, her companions and the
human race by the spread of a hostile alien species. But this
description hardly begins to capture their peculiar economy
of simplicity and power – the charismatic force of Weaver's
incarnation of Ripley's despairing but indomitable courage,
the uncanny otherness of the aliens, and of course the alien
universe itself, stripped of the clutter of social particularity to
reveal receding horizons of mythic significance. It now seems
as if it was clear from the outset that it would take more than
one film to explore those horizons, and thereby to unfold the
full meaning of Ripley's intimate loathing of her foes.

But there are, of course, more specific reasons for choosing
to focus on this series of films in a philosophical book on film
– reasons having to do with what one might call the underlying logic of the alien universe they depict. For these movies
are preoccupied, even obsessed, with a variety of interrelated
anxieties about human identity – about the troubled and
troubling question of individual integrity and its relation to
the body, sexual difference and nature. What exactly is my place

in nature? How far does the (natural) human ability to develop technology alienate us from the natural world? Am I (or am I in) my body? How sharply does my gender define me? How vulnerable does my body make me? Is sexual reproduction a threat to my integrity, and if so, does the reality and nature of that threat depend on whether I am a man or a woman? These are themes that emerge with almost mathematical elegance from the series' original conception of an alien species which involves human beings in the furtherance of its own reproductive cycle, and which thereby confronts its human protagonists with the flesh and blood basis of their existence. This issue – call it the relation of human identity to embodiment – has been central to philosophical reflection in the modern period since Descartes; but the sophistication and self-awareness with which these films deploy and develop that issue, together with a number of related issues also familiar to philosophers, suggest to me that they should themselves be taken as making real contributions to these intellectual debates. In other words, I do not look to these films as handy or popular illustrations of views and arguments properly developed by philosophers; I see them rather as themselves reflecting on and evaluating such views and arguments, as thinking seriously and systematically about them in just the ways that philosophers do. Such films are not philosophy's raw material, nor a source for its ornamentation; they are philosophical exercises, philosophy in action – film as philosophizing.

Furthermore, the 'Alien' series' interest in the bodily basis of human identity inexorably raises a number of interrelated questions about the conditions of cinema as such. For the medium is itself dependent upon the photographic reproduction (or better, transcription) of human beings, the projection of moving images of embodied human individuals presented to a camera. In one sense, in one frame of mind, this phenomenon can appear utterly banal; in another, it can seem utterly mysterious – as fascinating as the fact that a human being can be portrayed in paint, or that ink-marks on paper can express a thought. One might say that cinematic projections, with their unpredictable but undeniable capacity to translate (and to fail to translate) certain individual physiognomies into movie stardom, are one of the necessary possibilities to which embodied creatures such as ourselves are subject; and we cannot understand that subjection without understanding the nature of photographic transcription as such, hence without understanding what becomes of anything and everything on film.

These questions, about the nature of the cinematic medium, are perhaps those which we might expect any philosophical book on film to address – they are what is typically referred to when philosophers refer to 'the philosophy of film'; and this book does indeed find itself addressing such questions in a number of places. But it does so because it finds that these films themselves address such questions – because it finds that, in their reflections on human embodiment, they find themselves reflecting upon what makes it possible for them to engage in such reflections, upon the conditions for the possibility of film. In other words, a fundamental part of the philosophical work of these films is best understood as philosophy of film.

But the series has developed in such a way that its individual members have ineluctably been forced to grapple with a range of other conditions for their own possibility. To begin with, each film sits more or less uneasily within the genre of science fiction, with more or less strong ties in any individual case with the adjacent genres of horror, thriller, action, war and fantasy movies; and, although each film can be regarded as self-contained or self-sufficient, hence capable of being understood on its own terms, each succeeding film has also been created in clear awareness of its relation to its forebears. The distinctive character of each new episode in the series is thus in part a consequence of the increasingly complex nature of its thematic and narrative inheritance; but primarily it results from a commitment on the part of the series producers (Gordon Carroll, David Giler and Walter Hill) to find a new director for each episode, and preferably one with great potential rather than with an established cinematic track record. The series so far has used the talents, and helped to make or to consolidate the reputation, of Ridley Scott, James Cameron, David Fincher and Jean-Pierre Jeunet. Each episode can therefore be seen as an early step in the development of a highly influential and acclaimed cinematic career, and hence as internally related to such original and substantial fims as *Blade Runner*, *Terminator* and *Terminator 2*, *Se7en*, *Delicatessen* and *The City of Lost Children*.

This unique conjunction of circumstances means that a detailed study of the 'Alien' series will allow us, first, to examine the ways in which the specific conventions of traditional film genres, and the more general conditions of movie-making in Hollywood (as opposed, say, to those in the independent sector or in Europe), can both support and resist the achievement of artistic excellence. Here, what emerges in the coming chapters will confirm that, if we have not already done so, we can and should move beyond the disabling thought (a thought that can only disable genuine thoughtfulness about cinema) that artistic excellence is necessarily unobtainable in even the most unpromising of Hollywood contexts. Second, such a study also allows an investigation into the condition of sequeldom – a mode of movie-making that has appeared to dominate in Hollywood over the last decade, as if American commercial cinema had returned to one of its most influential early forms of the 1930s and 1940s, but in a much more self-conscious (sometimes serious, sometimes merely exploitative) way. An important issue here is the way in which a 'franchise' can renew itself over time, in part by explicitly reflecting upon what is involved in inheriting a particular set of characters in a particular narrative universe – the constraints and opportunities internal to (what, as a philosopher, I am inclined to call the logic of) that inheritance.

A third reason for studying this series is that each individual member of it is also an individual film in the series of a particularly gifted director's work. Each such movie can thus be studied as a point of intersection between a director's talents and artistic vision, and the narrative and thematic potential inherent in the alien universe; each film simultaneously unfolds more of the identity or individuality of its director and of its universe, as if each is made more itself in and through the complementarities and contrasts generated by their intense mutual engagement. In this way, we might be able to make some progress in understanding the general significance of (the insights made available, as well as the confusions engendered, by) our desire to talk of a film's director as its author, and hence to regard a film director's *oeuvre* as possessed of a particular thematic and artistic unity.

If, then, the developments of plot and character that make up the individual substance of these films can be thought of as generated by a reflective engagement with their own status as sequels, and hence with questions of inheritance and originality, then we could say that the series as a whole makes progress by reflecting upon the conditions of its own possibility. We might think of this kind of reflection as particularly demanded of any art in the condition of modernism – in which its own history (its inheritance of conventions, techniques and resources) has become an undismissable problem for it, something it can neither simply accept nor simply reject. But to make progress by reflecting upon the conditions of its own possibility is also as good a characterization as could be desired of the way in which any truly rigorous philosophy must proceed; for any philosophy that failed to engage in such reflection would fail to demand of itself what it makes it its business to demand of any and every other discipline with which it presumes to engage. Hence, as well as thinking of the 'Alien' series as an exemplary instance of cinematic modernism, we might also consider it as exemplary of cinema that finds itself in the condition of philosophy – of film as philosophy.

It is because I believe that these movies can be thought of in this way – as at once film as philosophizing, philosophy of film, and film in the condition of philosophy – that I regard myself as having written a philosophy book on film rather than a book about some films which happens to have some philosophy in it. And it is this same belief that leads me to regard the films under discussion in the following chapters in ways that differ fundamentally from the work of most of the film theorists I came across in preparing to write them. In the course of that preparation, it became clear to me that such theorists exhibit a strong tendency to treat the films they discuss as objects to which specific theoretical edifices (originating elsewhere, in such domains as psychoanalysis or political theory) could be applied. Even the most useful of these discussions would usually begin with a long explanation of the relevant theory, and turn to the specific film only at the end, and only as a cultural product whose specific features served to illustrate the truth of that theory – as one more phenomenon the theory rendered comprehensible. Of course, I have no objection to anyone making use of whatever intellectual resources they find pertinent in coming to understand a film's power and interest – I will be doing so myself, here and there, in the chapters to come.[1] However, the approaches I encountered seemed to me to lack any sense that the films themselves might have anything to contribute to our understanding of them – that they might contain a particular account of themselves, of why they are as they are, an account that might contribute to an intellectual exploration of the issues to which these pre-established bodies of theory also contribute, or even serve critically to evaluate those theories, to put their accuracy or exhaustiveness in question.

In short, such film theory as I have encountered tends to see in films only further confirmation of the truth of the theoretical machinery to which the theorist is already committed; the film itself has no say in what we are to make of it, no voice in the history of its own reception or comprehension. One of the reasons this book approaches questions about film through a detailed reading of specific films is precisely to put this tendency in question – to suggest that such films are in fact as capable of putting in question our prior faith in our general theories as they are of confirming that faith. This is, of course, just another way of saying that films can be seen to engage in systematic and sophisticated thinking about their themes and about themselves – that films can philosophize.

Reiterating such a claim about these films, these products of a lucrative Hollywood franchise in a popular commercial genre, might bring to the surface an anxiety that is very likely to emerge whenever a philosopher finds philosophizing going on in places where we tend not to expect it – isn't such an interpretation of these movies just a matter of over-interpretation, of reading things into them that simply aren't there? There is, of course, no general way of allaying such anxieties; whether or not a particular reading of a film in fact reads things into it as opposed to reading things out of it is not something that can be settled apart from a specific asessment of that reading against one's own assessment of the given film (and vice versa). Certainly, to think that my readings must be over-interpretations simply because they quickly find themselves grappling with questions that are of interest to philosophers would suggest a rather impoverished conception of the intellectual powers of film and of the pervasiveness of matters of philosophical interest in human life.

Nevertheless, this anxiety does accurately register something specific to these particular films – the fact that (in a manner I think of as bequeathed to them by one of their producers, Walter Hill) they appear to demand interpretation, and interpretation of a certain kind. From beginning to end, the 'Alien' films present us with small, isolated groups of human beings framed most immediately against the infinity of the cosmos. Each individual's inhabitation of the universe appears unmediated by the more complex interweavings of culture and society, those systems of signification which always already determine the meaning of any actions and events encompassed by them; their only carapace or exoskeleton is the bare minimum of technology necessary for their survival (whether an ore-carrying ship, an atmosphere processing facility, a waste refinery or a covert military/scientific research station). This cosmic backdrop makes it all but impossible to avoid grasping the narrative and thematic structure of the films in metaphysical or existential terms – as if the alien universe could not but concern itself with the human condition as such (as opposed to some specific inflection of that condition, some particular way in which a given human society has adapted, and adapted to, its environment, some individual way of making sense of its circumstances).

In choosing, as my disciplinary bent would anyway incline me, to meet these films' demand to be understood metaphysically, I do not take myself to be endorsing every element of that understanding (or even endorsing the understanding of philosophy as inherently metaphysical – as opposed, say, to thinking of it as aiming to diagnose or overcome the metaphysical). Neither do I take myself to be overlooking (or denying) the fact that any narrative universe designed to depict humanity *sub specie aeternitatis* will always exemplify a particular human way of making sense of ourselves and our circumstances – that any given metaphysics is culturally and socially specific, and hence that much of interest might emerge by asking how these films' metaphysical ambitions relate to the particular historical circumstances of their production.

But of course, choosing to plot those relations does not negate but rather presupposes a grasp of the relevant metaphysical ambitions; and by the same token, choosing to focus exclusively upon their metaphysical register does not at all commit me to the view that any other focus is misplaced or otiose. On the contrary, whilst I have attempted to provide a full or complete reading of the series' underlying (call it metaphysical) logic, in that I have aimed to establish a coherent perspective from which these films do genuinely form a series (a sequence in which each member appears as generated by its predecessor, and generative of its successor), I do not regard that reading as exhaustive or exclusive – as if its validity entails the invalidity of any alternative readings or approaches to reading, of any claims to identify another (metaphysical or non-metaphysical) kind of coherence in their individual and collective identity. The validity of any such claims rather turns, to say it once again, on specific assessments of their bearing on our specific experiences of the films themselves (and vice versa).

All that this book implicitly claims is that philosophy has something distinctive to contribute to the ongoing conversations about particular films and the medium of cinema that play such an important role in contemporary public culture. Philosophy's voice has a specific register, one that distinguishes it even from that of film theory and cultural studies; but in making itself heard, it has (and needs to have) no desire to render other voices mute.

The overall structure of this little book takes the form of four chapters. Each is concerned with one episode in the 'Alien' series, but each also looks in detail at other work by the director of that episode – sometimes only one other film, sometimes more. The first chapter develops at some length my understanding of the basic logic of the alien universe; the other three are more preoccupied with the artistic problems and possibilities they pose, as well as the incitements and resistances they generate, for the directors who follow Ridley Scott. The fourth chapter, on *Alien Resurrection*, functions as a conclusion that is also a prologue, since this episode in the series is itself most knowingly constructed as a meditation upon the degree to which any such series can successfully renew itself, and thus places the further continuation of the series in question whilst at the same time suggesting that its potential for continuation can survive the most thoroughgoing attempts (as, for example, in *Alien*[3]) to exhaust or foreclose its narrative possibilities.

I would like to thank Simon Critchley and Richard Kearney for inviting me to contribute a volume to this series, Tony Bruce at Routledge for helping to develop and support such a worthwhile publishing venture, Philip Wheatley and Alison Baker for reading and offering comments on the whole of this book in manuscript, and a number of anonymous readers for Routledge whose responses also helped to improve the text. The portion of chapter one devoted to *Blade Runner* is a much-revised version of an article that first appeared in *Film and Philosophy*, Volume 1, 1994.

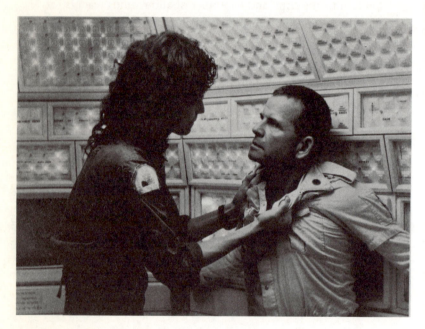

Alien © 1979 20th Century-Fox Film. Reproduced by courtesy of the Roland Grant Archive.

Kane's Son, Cain's Daughter:
Ridley Scott's *Alien*

One

Above the sparse opening credits, as the camera pans slowly from the outer rim of a planet's Saturnian rings across the pitch black of its surface and back out to the opposite rim of those rings, the title of this film is indicated in a slowly emerging sequence of vertical strokes. It thus appears to emerge from the surface of the planet itself, the place from which the alien creature after which the film is named emerges; and it is indicated rather than spelt out, because some of its constituent letters (not being wholly composed of (near) vertical strokes) are rather implied or suggested, their precise identity left for the viewer to determine in her imagination – just as this film's director will leave implicit the overall appearance and exact nature of the alien creature itself until (and in some respects beyond) its end. Perhaps, then, we should not expect the exact nature of this film to be any less alien to us than its eponymous protagonist – any less unpredictable from what we think we know that a science fiction or horror movie must be, any less unaccommodated by our existing sense of what the medium of film as such can allow or achieve.

Next, the camera watches the enormous expanse of the Nostromo approach and pass by, with its substantial command module utterly dwarfed by the industrial landscape of domed cylinders and stackpipes (containing 20,000,000 tonnes of mineral ore) in tow behind it. We cut to the interior of the ship: the camera reveals an octagonal corridor, neither spacious nor oppressive, then turns to look down its junction with another corridor; it pans unhurriedly across a table in a communal area, then down another corridor to a space cluttered with monitor screens and banks of instruments. There is movement – the flutter of paper in a draught, the dipping head of a toy bird – but it is mechanical, devoid of human significance. Then one of the display screens lights up as a computer begins to chatter; we see downscrolling symbols reflected in the visor of a helmet. As the ship absorbs and reacts to this burst of activity, we cut to a doorway: coats flutter in the draught induced by the doors as they open, and the camera takes us into a blindingly white, sterile room, dominated by an array of glass-lidded coffin-shaped modules, each oriented towards a central stem, like the petals of a flower. The lids rise, to reveal a number of human bodies: in a series of stately but fluid dissolves, we see one of them sit up, remove a monitor pad, and stand up. He is wearing a loincloth or a pair of shorts, the whiteness of the material combining with that of the room to accentuate the pallor of his skin, its distance from the warm, rosy pink we think of as the appropriate colour for human flesh; his eyes are closed, he rubs his face, as if unwillingly acceding to consciousness. His face – deeply lined and weary, marked by some kind of suffering from which it has not yet escaped – is instantly recognizable as that of John Hurt, whose name was perhaps the most famous of those which appeared during the film's opening credits. We think we have finally arrived at the human centre of the film that is about to begin.

And we are wrong (as we are wrong in taking Janet Leigh's character to be the protagonist of *Psycho*). But we have been shown a great deal in this prologue that is true to what will follow, true both to this director and to his tale (as written by Dan O'Bannon). The slow, calm, controlled movements of the camera have established the basic rhythm of the direction – unhurried but supremely confident that what we will eventually be shown will be worthy of our investment of interest. We can also see Scott's confidence in his sets and special effects, even in the wake of 2001 and *Star Wars*: they can bear up under close scrutiny in the absence of human activity, and thus make more credible the normalcy or every-dayness of that activity when it finally begins. This is not a cartoon or fantasy of space technology and interstellar travel; it is a working ship in the real world of the human future – a world quickly shown to have inherited our predilection for social hierarchy and salary disputes, whose bickering inhabitants can barely summon an interest in their fellows or themselves.

Beyond this, the camera's unhurried scrutiny of the *Nostromo's* empty spaces points up the imperturbable self-sufficiency of the ship, its ability to guide itself safely across interstellar distances in the complete absence of conscious human control. This subtly inflects our sense of the relative dependence of human beings and their technological tools. When the crew finally emerge from their ship's hibernation pods so that they can respond to the unidentified radio beacon signal, the ship's need for them in these unusual circumstances only emphasizes their superfluity in normal circumstances. They appear as useful creatures for the ship's purposes, as if a kind of pet or parasite, and the significance of their own purposes and fate is correspondingly diminished. Indeed, when we come to realize that the planet and the ship of the prologue constitute the whole of the coming narrative's locations, and hence that we have been shown the entire terrain of the film before its inhabitation by character and narrative, as if demonstrating the world's continuation beyond our participation in or knowledge of it, this prologue underlines the essential belatedness and relativity of human concerns, their insignificance in the face of the universe which makes them possible.

Most important of all, however, is the complex manner of the crew's entry into consciousness, and into their own story. On one level, the suddenly deadened soundtrack and sequence of overlapping dissolves that chart Hurt's emergence into conscious awareness seem to mimic the mode of that emergence – as disorganized and disorienting as his first perceptions appear to be to him, as if he were awaking from a dream. But it could, of course, equally well characterize the process of beginning to dream, of being translated from consciousness to that mode of awareness in which nightmares come; and we have already been shown that nightmare landscape, the source and context of their coming trials. On another level, the crew appears to be undergoing a kind of rebirth.[1] They emerge like seeds from a pod, as if extruded by the ship itself, almost as naked as they day they were born; and Hurt's dazed face registers the impact of the world on his senses as if for the first time. However, his umbilical cord is a monitor pad and line, the pallor of his body is barely distinguishable from the sterile whiteness of his technological womb, and his sexual organs are covered over; and the presentation of these details through a silenced soundtrack and overlapping dissolves, with their subversion of the conditions of ordinary perceptual experience, now suggest a displacement of reality not by dream but by fantasy. We are being given a picture of human origination that represses its creatureliness, that represents parturition as an automated function of technology rather than of flesh emerging noisily and painfully from flesh – as essentially devoid of blood, trauma and sexuality.

Does this fantasy originate in the director, or in the characters themselves, or in the society to which they are returning? Does it represent a consummation devoutly to be wished, or (given the scene's conjunction of this fantasy's realization with the onset of nightmare) are we rather meant to see that the monstrousness of life is not so easily to be avoided? It is, at any rate, umbilically linked to the nightmare that is about to penetrate and overwhelm the *Nostromo*.

THE ALIEN CYCLE OF LIFE

How is it that *Alien* transforms itself slowly but surely from a pure science fiction film into a horror movie, or rather into a highly original hybrid of the two? Why is it that the alien inspires – in the *Nostromo*'s crew and in us – not only fear and terror, but horror? Stanley Cavell has suggested one way of discriminating between these responses, by discriminating between those aspects of the world to which they respond:

> Fear is of danger; terror is of violence, of the violence I might do or that might be done me. I can be terrified of thunder, but not horrified by it. And isn't it the case that not the human horrifies me, but the inhuman, the monstrous? Very well. But only what is human can be inhuman. – Can only the human be monstrous? If something is monstrous, and we do not believe that there are monsters, then only the human is a candidate for the monstrous.
>
> If only humans feel horror (if the capacity to feel horror is a development of the specifically human biological inheritance), then maybe it is a response specifically to being human. To what, specifically, about being human? Horror is the title I am giving to the perception of the precariousness of human identity, to the perception that it

may be lost or invaded, that we may be, or may become, something other than we are, or take ourselves for; that our origins as human beings need accounting for, and are unaccountable.[2]

This is why the monster in horror movies is so often a zombie or one of the living dead, a vampire, a botched creation, construction or reconstruction of the human – this is why Frankenstein's monster is prototypical of the genre. As well as threatening to inflict a peculiarly intimate, distorting or rending violence upon vulnerable human flesh and blood (a threat repeatedly carried out in this film and its successors), these creatures are themselves mutations or distortions of the human. What, then, of Ridley Scott's alien; what precisely is it about the precariousness of our own human identity that we see in the monstrosity of this monster?

Beyond the threat of violence that this dragon, as big as a man, represents (and to which terror rather than horror is the primary response), there stands first the alien's motive for inflicting that violence upon the human beings who encounter it. For it harbours no general or specific malice against the human race as such, or against the crew of the *Nostromo*. It attaches itself to, and exits from, Kane's body because this is dictated by its mode of reproduction: it can grow only within another living being. And it attacks the rest of the crew because they threaten its survival (hence, at least initially, that of its species) and because they represent the only available means for the continued existence of that species. It is, in short, just doing what comes naturally to any species – following the imperatives of nature.

However, the alien species appears not so much to follow nature's imperatives as to incarnate them. This is not because it is driven to survive and reproduce, but rather because it is so purely driven, because it appears to have no other drives – no desire to communicate, no culture, no modes of play or pleasure or industry other than those necessitated by its own continuation as a species. The alien's form of life is (just, merely, simply) life, life as such: it is not so much a particular species as the essence of what it means to be a species, to be a creature, a natural being – it is Nature incarnate or sublimed, a nightmare embodiment of the natural realm understood as utterly subordinate to, utterly exhausted by, the twinned Darwinian drives to survive and reproduce.

The alien's monstrosity derives further specificity from the fact that its mode of reproduction is parasitic. After seeing it burst from Kane's torso, we realize that neither the planet nor the alien ship from which the creature emerged is its true home: we recall the fossilized remains of a member of another alien species encountered within that ship (seated behind what looked like an enormous weapon) with a hole punched through its chest, and realize that the ship's cargo of eggs was no more indigenous to the ship itself than it is to the desolate planet upon which that ship crash-landed – indeed, that the crash-landing itself might well have been induced by the parasitic alien species' progressive infestation of that ship's crew. This parasitism is an extreme manifestation of the relationship any species has with the broader system of nature: it signifies at once their vulnerability to predation by the other species with which they must inhabit the natural realm, and their dependence upon their environment for sustenance. Metaphysically, it represents a perception of life itself as something external to or other than the species which incarnate it – something that invades, makes use of, and then discards, any and every manifestation of itself, as if living beings are merely its vehicles, slaves or hosts. The alien's parasitism exemplifies the essential parasitism of Nature; it represents the radical lack of autonomy that is of the essence of creaturehood – its need to incorporate, and its openness to incorporation by, that which is not itself, and its victimization by the life within it.

However, perhaps the most uncanny aspect of the alien's monstrosity is determined by the specific mode of its parasitism. For, in order to reproduce, it must insert a long, flexible member into the host's body through one of that body's orifices, and deposit a version of itself within its host's torso where it develops to the point at which it must force itself out again. In short, what happens to Kane is that he is impregnated with an alien foetus which his body then brings to term and labours to bring forth into the world; he undergoes a nightmare vision of sexual intercourse, pregnancy and birth. The heart of the alien's monstrosity is thus that it relates itself to its host species in a manner which embodies a particular fantasy of sexual relations between human males and human females. The threat stalking the corridors and ducts of the *Nostromo* is thus a vision of masculinity *and* femininity, hence of sexual difference as such, as monstrous. The monster itself is the incarnation of masculinity, understood as penetrative sexual violence; but as such, it threatens the human race as a whole with the monstrous fate of feminization, forcing our species to occupy the sexual role (that of being violated, of playing host to a parasite, and of facing death in giving birth) that women are imagined to occupy in relation to men.

This thought about the monster's uncanny parasitism is not contradicted, but is rather made more specific, if we further note its intensely oral focus. In this respect, of course, the alien's mode of parasitism reflects its general mode of being;

for at every stage of its post-partum development, it presents itself to us as all mouth. From the metallic incisors of the near-blind chestburster to the teeth-within-teeth of the warrior, it is as if its nature finds its fullest expression in images of devouring insatiability (and the threat such images pose for men and for women might be taken to be as different, in nature and in depth, as are the threat of castration and that of an infant's limitless demands on its mother). But the facehugger variant of this being that is all mouth also chooses to penetrate the mouths of its victims when impregnating them; and on the assumption that its mode of reproduction is a monstrous image of the human mode of reproduction, this implies that to occupy the role of women in relation to men is to have one's mouth stopped or gagged, to be rendered mute (a muteness registered in the long wastes of silence on this film's soundtrack, and in its sense that any form of negotiation – any conversation or intercourse – with the alien species is utterly beside the point). Heterosexual masculinity here appears as aiming to silence the woman's voice, to deny her the most fundamental expression of her individuality. For the human race to be feminized is thus for human individuality as such to be threatened, as if the alien's monstrosity declares that something about the acknowledgement of individuality (in particular, acknowledging the relation of individuality to sexual difference) sticks in our throats, makes us gag.

What holds these various facets of the alien's monstrousness together is their relation to human fantasies and fears about human embodiment or animality: collectively, they give expression to an idea of ourselves as victimized by our own flesh and blood – as if it is essentially other than, alien to, what we are, as if our bodies not only made us vulnerable to suffering and death, but made our very humanness precarious.

Sexual difference, the drive to survive and reproduce, dependence upon and vulnerability to the natural world: these are all aspects of our creaturely life, features brought to an unprecedented pitch of purity in the alien species but common nevertheless to both human and alien, and yet experienced as monstrous. The alien thus represents the return of the repressed human body, of our ineluctable participation in the realm of nature – of life.

A further aspect of the alien's incarnation of nature also serves to subvert one our most familiar ways of repressing our own creaturehood, of understanding our humanness as other to our embodiment. For this alien, is, of course, uniquely well-equipped to defend itself; or rather, with its leathery, indefinitely-fertile eggs, its foetal teeth and tail, the molecular acid it uses for blood and its capacity to transform its own skin into polarized silicone body-armour, it is its own survival equipment. It has internalized or become its own array of defensive and offensive tools and instruments – its flesh is armour and its blood a weapon; in short, its body is its technology. The alien thereby represents a mode of evolution that is not dwarfed by or in thrall to (say, alienated from) its technology, as the crew of the *Nostromo* appear to be; and more specifically, it undercuts our tendency to imagine that our social and cultural development, our ability to evolve beyond the limitations of the body by evolving tools and technology (to reduce our vulnerability and improve upon our natural powers), is the means by which we transcend our naturalness rather than a further expression of it, simply the exploitation of the biological endowment that is distinctive of our species. The alien's monstrously intimate incorporation of its technology into its nature is a projection of our horror at the thought that culture as such is in fact our second nature – not something other to our naturalness in which our humanity might safely reside, something from which we must accordingly think of our incarnate selves as alienated, on pain of annihilating our humanity.

RIPLEY AND ASH

It seems clear, however, that it is the alien's monstrous representation of human sexual difference that most fundamentally drives the plot of Scott's film. For given the alien's threatening incarnation of predatory masculinity, and its attempt to locate the human as such in the position of femininity, it is only to be expected that the heroic human protagonist of the drama that unfolds on board the *Nostromo* should turn out to be a woman rather than a man, and that of the two female candidates for this role, it should be Ripley rather than Lambert. Thus one of Scott's most effective subversions of the hybrid genre in which he is working (his association of femininity with heroism rather than victimhood) turns out to be dictated by the logic of his monster's monstrousness. Hence our sense that Ripley's final, isolated confrontation with the alien is not accidental or merely a generic twist but more profoundly satisfying – something to which she is fated.

Certainly, no other member of the crew is as sensitive as Ripley to the risks attaching to the alien's penetration of their second, external or technological, skin – the ship itself; only Ash's insubordination (his refusal to attend to her voice over the intercom) overcomes her rooted determination to keep the stricken Kane outside the airlock. And in her climactic struggle with the alien once it has entered the ship, she succeeds in ejecting it from the shuttle only because she immediately protects herself from it by getting into a spacesuit. The strength and orientation of Ripley's instincts here are best understood as giving expression to her instinctive familiarity with, her subconscious inhabitation of, the conception of femininity in its relation to masculinity that underpins the alien's monstrousness. She acts consistently from the outset to preserve the physical integrity of the ship she briefly commands because she has all along understood her own femaleness in the terms that the alien seeks to impose upon the human species, and hence has always understood her body as a vessel whose integrity must at all costs be preserved.

The alien's distinctive mode of parasitic predation is profoundly shocking to the men in the crew, to whom a female subject position – one of vulnerability to rape, impregnation and giving birth – is essentially alien and traumatizing. It is no less so to the only other woman in the crew (Lambert), who – whilst sharing Ripley's innate caution – is happy to risk the integrity of the ship when she needs to re-enter it, and who is rendered powerless when that integrity is violated. The scene of her death, in which she seems hypnotized by the alien, which is there given its most explicitly sexualized repertoire of gestures (its prehensile tail shown creeping between her legs), suggests that the predatory aspect of masculinity is either too unfamiliar to her, or perhaps in a certain sense too familiar,[3] to be gainsaid. On the deepest psychic level, such male monstrosity is no surprise to Ripley at all; it is rather a confirmation of her basic view of the human world of sexual difference, and an opportunity for her to act upon her long-matured comprehension of how best to oppose its essential monstrosity – by doing whatever it might take to avoid the violation of heterosexual intercourse. In short, extending a long-familiar mythological trope, Ripley's emergence as the human hero of this tale is empowered or underwritten by her implied celibacy; her refusal to submit to the alien's advances has been long-prepared by, is in a sense the apotheosis of, her resolute virginity.

On one level, of course, the purity of her resolution here is precisely what makes her a match for the pure hostility of the alien: she is as profoundly attuned to, and as psychologically well-equipped for, survival as the alien itself – and this is perhaps the germ from which the developing interest of the other films in the series, in presenting Ripley and her alien opponent as somehow made for one another (as if each sees the other as its equal or as itself), can be seen in retrospect to have evolved. At the same time, however, what – mythologically speaking – endows Ripley with her drive for survival is her equally resolute repression of her drive to reproduce; and in this respect, she exists in utter opposition to the alien's incarnation of that drive. In other words, to become capable and worthy of vanquishing her opponent, she must sever the connection between femaleness, heterosexual intercourse and fertility – she must, in short, deny her body's openness to maternity. This severance is tracked most explicitly by the film in its representation of Ripley's relationship to the sole embodiment of the maternal principle in the *Nostromo* – the ship's computer that the crew all refer to as 'Mother'.

Like the rest of the crew, Ripley is reborn by Mother from the ship's technological womb in order to embark on a mission to locate and bring back a member of the alien species, a goal in relation to which her life is deemed utterly expendable: it is as if Mother is prepared to sacrifice the offspring of her own fertility in order to secure the cosmic embodiment of fertility as such. When, after Kane's and Dallas' deaths, Ripley gains direct access to Mother, she uncovers this programmed malevolence – and in so doing, she unleashes upon herself a near-lethal attack from Ash. Against this background, it can seem rather more than accidental that her final plan for bringing about the alien's destruction should involve the destruction of the ship itself, and hence of the ship's computer; and when Mother prevents her from aborting that countdown, as if refusing to attend at once to her words and her needs, Ripley herself is clear that this is more than a merely mechanical failure: her response is to scream at Mother – 'You bitch!' – and attempt to smash the central computer console.

Does this description simply collude with Ripley's paranoia? Should we dismiss her sense of personal victimization by a machine as a hysterical but understandable confusion between the true villains (the Company who formulated the computer's instructions) and their unthinking instruments? But on a Darwinian conception of things, is it not of the essence of Mother Nature's fecundity that its individual offspring be seen as the expendable vehicles for the survival and reproduction of the species they instantiate, and that those individual species be seen as expendable vehicles for the survival and repro-duction of life as such? In this sense, fertility has only its own reproduction as a goal; hence, children must conceive of themselves as reducible to expressions of and sacrifices to the motherhood of their mothers; and women must conceive of motherhood as reducing them to a vehicle for and a sacrifice to the cosmic principle of fertility.

Hence, Ripley's extreme detestation of Mother and mother-hood, and her extreme detestation of the alien and its predatory parasitism, are at root responsive to the same phenomenon. The condition of maternity involves a double parasitism, because the woman's body becomes host not just to another individual being but to the principle of fecundity as such. To be a mother means becoming a vehicle for life – sacrificing one's physical and spiritual integrity to a blind, mechanical force in relation to which nothing (no particular member of a species, and no particular species) has any intrinsic significance. In short, Mother is a bitch because life is a bitch.

It is, however, worth remembering that Scott does suggest at least a vestigial nostalgia or yearning for maternity on Ripley's part – when he presents her as risking her own safety and the destruction of the alien in order to rescue Jones, the ship's cat. This animal not only becomes the object of a displaced expression of Ripley's maternal impulse; it is also, of course, a representation of nonhuman life coexisting in fruitful symbiosis with human beings, and hence provides the shadow of a suggestion that the life of the cosmos is not utterly inimical to human flourishing. The fact that Ripley can more easily allow this impulse to find expression in relation to a nonhuman animal does not exactly subvert her hostility to her own fertility; but it does provide a vital opening for James Cameron's rewriting of Scott's broader vision of the essential monstrousness of human fertility and sexuality in *Aliens*.

Nevertheless, within that broader vision, Scott reinforces Ripley's detestation of motherhood by opposing it to Ash's uncanny attunement with Mother. Ash is, at the outset of the film, the first to respond to Mother's request to speak to Dallas; he runs his continuing task of data-collation in parallel with Mother's, and is the crew member most comfortable with the computational instrumentation that Mother provides for their well-being; he is the only one who was always aware of the true purpose of their mission, and is able to attack Ripley in the computer room because he has his own private means of access to Mother.

And yet, of course, Ash is not himself the offspring of a human mother; he is an android. This constitutes his deepest mode of connection with Mother, but it makes that connection paradoxical in the sense that an essentially asexual being, whose body is composed of circuitry and silicone rather than flesh and blood, should be so intimately identified in this film with maternity, and hence with fertility and nature. This paradox is deepened by the degree of Ash's identification with the alien: he implicitly guides the expedition to locate the alien eggs, he brings about its entry into the *Nostromo*, he protects it against the crew's efforts to kill it (holding back Parker from attacking it when it gives birth to itself from Kane's chest, providing a highly unreliable set of tools to track it), and his final words to the crew give explicit expression to his admiration for its purity – for the way its structural perfection as an organism is matched only by its hostility, unclouded by conscience or considerations of morality. Most explicitly, when he attacks Ripley, in defence of the alien and on Mother's behalf, he tries to choke her by inserting a rolled-up magazine into her mouth – thus identifying himself with the alien's violation of the human body and voice. In other words, the inorganic Ash is as deeply attracted to the alien's incarnation of the essence of the organic as he is attuned to Mother's sterile realization of fertility.

The film suggests two ways of understanding this apparent paradox. First, recalling its earlier depictions of the cosmic life principle as somehow external or other to the organic realm, we can infer that the asexual circuitry of Ash and his Mother are intended to represent life as such as not itself alive, essentially not animal or fleshly, but rather a matter of codes and programming. Life as such is the non-organic, super-mechanical, blind determinism that drives the organic realm – call it the codedness of the genetic code. Hence, even when it is fantasized as denuded of animality, of flesh and blood (as in the film's opening technological phantasm of birth), its essence (as unfolded to Ripley in Mother's indifference and Ash's murderousness) is no less death-dealing than in its alien incarnation (that incarnation of carnality as such, of life's code made pure flesh). Whether it is conceived of as the alien other of flesh or as its sublime essence, life is monstrous.

The second way of understanding the paradox turns on Ash's primary role or function in the crew – he is the science officer, and hence the person most thoroughly dedicated to the study and comprehension of nature. His inorganic status here symbolizes much that our culture imagines of the scientist – that he be purely rational, in a way untainted by considerations of emotion, personal opinion or prejudice, or the claims of morality; but also that he be endowed with an overwhelming admiration or awe for the object of his study, a sense of wonder in response to nature and the cosmos. Hence his empathy for the alien, that incarnation of animate matter and animality, the perfect organism. For Ash, beyond its significance as the objective of the mission he has been programmed to take on, the alien symbolizes the true significance of the cosmic principle of life; it signifies the essential insignificance of human morality and culture, and indeed of the human race as such – the fact that we are not at the centre of the universe and its concerns. His willingness to regard the crew of the *Nostromo* as expendable thus encapsulates a vision of science as essentially amoral or inhuman, not just in that its search for the truth about nature demands that human values be set aside in favour of objectively establishing the facts, but also in that the truth about nature that science reveals is that nature is itself fundamentally amoral or inhuman. Both Ash and his Mother identify themselves with life as such, not with human life and human concerns – after all, they are not themselves incarnations of human life. Little wonder that we feel obscurely satisfied with this film's presentation of the ship's science officer as an inhuman being at one with the monster.

My account thus far leaves implicit one other suggestive dimension of the identification of science with the alien. For when Ash imitates the alien's distinctive parasitic violation of the human body in forcing a rolled-up magazine down Ripley's throat, the pictures on the wall around him suggest that it is a pornographic publication; his actions thereby underline the film's equation of the alien with masculine sexual violence, but they also imply an identification of science with masculinity. The idea is that scientific approaches to nature are in effect violent, an attempt to penetrate or violate the natural realm, as if emotionally neutered and morally neutral observation of and experimentation with nature amounts to its rape. But since Ash is represented as identifying with the essence of the natural realm he is devoted to observing, his essentially masculine sexual violence further implies that the cosmic life-principle as such should be understood, for all its ambivalent externality to the organic realm, as essentially masculine – as if the drive for reproduction is rapacious, inherently violent and violating.

This vision of the cosmos as unstoppable fecundity and endless self-overcoming might be related to certain aspects of Nietzsche's early, Dionysian vision of what he later calls the will-to-power – the capacity to impose form on the formlessness of chaos, and to destroy or sacrifice any given form in the name of another, newer such form. It is an idea of life as an endless becoming, but according to which fitness for life is a matter of an individual's or a species' ability to impose itself not only on its environment but (when necessary) upon itself – for instance, by reinventing itself so as to accommodate any irresistible changes in that environment, or to rescue itself from the rigor mortis of stability or stasis, from mere self-repetition. Hence the film's emphasis upon the alien's plasticity – its unceasing evolution from one phase or mode of being to another, and its capacity to adapt and defend itself against the most extreme environmental circumstances within the span of its individual life cycle.

Of course, one might read such an identification of the scientific method and its object of study with male rapacity in another way – to suggest that a vision of nature as essentially will-to-power is not a revelation of nature's essence but rather a distorting interpretation of nature that gives expression to the masculine sexual violence implicit in the scientific approach that generates it. However, the film's presentation of Ripley's almost undeviating resistance to its central symbols of life understood as will-to-power (whether in the form of heterosexual intercourse, the attentions and intentions of Ash and Mother, or the parasitism of the alien) as essentially heroic appears rather to underwrite her perception of fertility or maternity as a violation or rape of femininity, of maternity as demanding an alien inhabitation of her flesh rather than as allowing its fulfilment. It is as if life itself really is to be understood as an inherently masculine assault upon women, in which they function merely as the means for the onward transmission of something (an intrinsically penetrating and aggressive force, or drive, or will) essentially alien to them.

Ripley's unremitting drive to preserve her integrity is thus, in essence, an expression of her sense of alienation from life, nature and the cosmos, and from everything in herself that participates in – that binds her ineluctably to – that which she hates so purely. For after all, does she not in the end succeed in imposing her will upon Ash, Mother and the alien itself? Is not her final victory over the monster in the *Narcissus* (the

Nostromo's shuttle), her success in creating a space from which to give voice to the mayday message that she speaks over the film's concluding frames, achieved by reshaping her environment (making it a vacuum) and herself (suiting up) so that she might bury a harpoon in the heart of her opponent and in the heart of the heartless cosmos into which her weapon dispatches it? What better exemplification of the masculine will-to-power of which her thoughts, deeds and underlying psychology declare such detestation (as if the alien she confronts in the *Narcissus* is a reflection of herself)? (Seeing this beautifully choreographed assault, this seamless dovetailing of heart, mind and spirit in the service of vengeance, we might recall Ash's description of the alien – immediately after it has burst from Kane's chest – as 'Kane's son'. This is the film's most explicit reference to the alien's unmanning capacity to make human males pregnant; but its aural reference to the Bible's name for the first human murderer further implies that the monster's death-dealing rapacity is not essentially alien to humanity, but rather at work in the first human family, and never eradicated from the human family as such thereafter. If, then, Ripley is a sister under the skin to Kane's son, she is Cain's daughter – offspring not of God's beloved Abel but of his wrathful brother, the first violator of human solidarity, condemned by God to be a fugitive and vagabond on the earth, essentially not at home in the universe He created.) But if what Ripley hates is what saves her from what she hates (if it is the pure flame of the life in her that overcomes its own monstrous, externalized incarnation), must she end by hating herself, by overcoming that which she hates in herself, or by overcoming her hatred?

Developing answers to these questions will govern the evolution of the 'Alien' series in the hands of other directors; but it also governs the thematic structure and narrative development of Ridley Scott's next film – *Blade Runner*. For this film (written by Hampton Fancher and David Peoples) is explicitly concerned with the question of what it is to be human; more precisely, it is obsessed with it – obsessed in the way the leader of the replicants is obsessed with his quest for life, for a life which is on a par with that of human beings. To show that Roy Baty misconceives this quest as one for *more* life – as if a replicant might become human by living longer – is the goal of the film.

Like Ash, the replicants have no flesh and blood mother – but unlike Ash, they find this deeply traumatizing (a question about his feelings for his mother is what occasions the replicant Leon's opening murder of Deckard's colleague). This appears to be because (again unlike Ash) the replicants are not androids but rather products of genetic engineering destined for dangerous or dirty tasks in off-world colonies – hence are themselves composed of flesh and blood. As if to underline this, the film's relentless violence (quite apart from three 'retirements', we witness an attempted strangulation, savage beatings, an attack with an iron bar, deliberately broken fingers and a climax of concentrated physical suffering) is typically[4] directed towards replicants, as if to confront the authorities' doctrine that such embodied beings are incapable of suffering, are entities upon whom the infliction of pain is not a crime.

What these scenes instead elicit is an instinctive response to this treatment of the replicants which matches our response to such treatment of human beings; we see their behaviour as expressive of pain and suffering rather than as an empty

exhibition by automata. As Roy puts it: 'We're not computers
. . . we're physical'; the violence inflicted upon them estab-
lishes beyond political or philosophical debate that the
replicants are capable of manifesting the essential range and
complexity of feeling open to any human being. The empathic
claim their pain-behaviour makes upon us is what grounds
the film's assumption that it is this aspect of the replicants'
embodiment which is pertinent to their call for human
status, not that of whether anything *occupies* their bodies. *Blade
Runner* thus rejects any understanding of the human mind
or soul as hidden behind, entirely distinct from, the human
body. In presenting us with entities whose embodied life has
a complexity and range comparable to that of a human being,
Scott brings his viewers to apply to them the full range of
psychological concepts which constitute the logical space
of the mental, and thereby demonstrates that our attribution
of a mind to a given creature is a response to the behavioural
repertoire with which their particular embodiment endows
them. Wittgenstein once remarked that 'The human body is the
best picture of the human soul'; this film dramatizes and
projects that insight.

If, however, we are thereby given everything we need to
know – indeed, everything there is to know – about the
replicants which is relevant to their claim for human status,
if we (and anyone in the world of the film) can see that
nothing counts against their being treated as human, how and
why do most of the human beings in the film apparently fail
to see this? Why, for example, does Deckard's superior, Bryant
– the commander of the replicant-hunting blade runner
unit – regard the replicants as skin-jobs? The film's answer is
to be found in the fact that Bryant is 'the kind of lawman who
used to call black men "niggers"'; for nothing counts against

the replicants being treated as human except the unwillingness or refusal of other human beings to do so. No accumulation of facts or testimony of the senses can compel someone to acknowledge behaviour that fulfils all the criteria of pain-behaviour as the genuine expression of another human being's pain. Bryant's failure to acknowledge the replicants as human is not based on ignorance or repression of these facts, but is rather the expression of one possible attitude towards them. It follows that the humanity of the replicants is in the hands of their fellows; their accession to human status involves their being acknowledged as human by others, and if their humanity is denied, it withers. And in this respect, of course, they once again resemble the human beings who acknowledge or fail to acknowledge them.[5]

This theme is central to the film's depiction of the relationship between Deckard and Rachel. Their first meeting takes place across a Voight-Kampff (V-K) machine, the equipment used by blade runners to assess a subject's capillary dilation, blush response, fluctuation of the pupil, pheromone discharge and other physiological registers of emotional response – the theory being that replicants lack any empathic attunement with others and thereby betray their difference from human beings. As Tyrell, the designer of the replicants, points out, however, this lack of empathy and its correlative emotional immaturity is determined by the decision of the replicant's makers to restrict their lifespan to four years, and correspondingly constrain the range of their memories and experiences. Rachel, by contrast, has been gifted with a past that creates a cushion or pillow for the emotions, but which entails that she does not know that she is a replicant.

Deckard at first sees her failure to pass the V-K test as a simple proof of her nonhumanity, oblivious to that fact that his difficulty in detecting the usual emotional absence in her suggests rather that this lack is contingent, and a matter of degree, i.e. that the replicants might rather be seen as children in an emotional sense through no fault of their own, and thus as capable of maturity, and that some uncontroversially human beings (like Bryant) never attain such maturity.

His denial of Rachel's humanity intensifies when, in his apartment, he wrenches away the pillow of her past, reciting to her face the memories that make up her inner life and informing her of their 'true' origin (Tyrell's niece); even his attempts to back away from his brutality in the face of her pain are so clumsy as to suggest an inability to care sufficiently about her to do so with any consideration. Even after she saves him from Leon's murderous attack, his declaration that he would never personally hunt her down is based on the thought that he owes her one – that they are equals only in the way a debtor and his creditor are equals. When Rachel responds to this by asking whether Deckard has ever taken the V-K test himself, Scott invites us to acknowledge that a refusal to acknowledge another's humanity constitutes a denial of the humanity in oneself.

Deckard's redeemability is, however, revealed later in the same scene, when – after finding Rachel at the piano, playing because she cannot even trust her memory of piano lessons – he says 'You play beautifully'. The tact and delicacy of this prepare the ground for a full acknowledgement of their feelings for one another; but Deckard again mishandles things. Aware that Rachel now feels incapable of staking her life on her emotions, and hence of acknowledging her attraction to Deckard, he aims to help her overcome this anxiety; but he does so by pushing her back against the wall and dictating her expression of her feelings ('Say "Kiss me" . . . "I want you"

. . . Again . . .'). The fact that she then goes on to improvise expressions of her own ('Put your hands on me') does not make this initial forcing of words into her mouth any less disturbing a piece of sexual violence.

Deckard's actual redemption is made plain in the film's concluding sequence, when he returns to his apartment to find Rachel lying covered in a shroud-like sheet on the couch. But when he removes that covering, he finds a way of addressing her which brings her fully (back) to life. In their previous encounter, they faced one another standing, giving the scene a strong vertical patterning which emphasized Deckard's superior height, strength and aggression; now, he leans over her face from the head of the couch, creating an equally strong horizontal patterning which does away with his physical superiority and suggests that their profiles are complementary. The ensuing dialogue matches this sense of achieved equality: for Deckard now does not dictate Rachel's dialogue but asks her questions ('Do you love me . . . Do you trust me?') to which she is free to respond as she pleases, and to which she freely responds in the affirmative. Thus, by creating the terms for a conversation in which Rachel could freely acknowledge her love for him, he acknowledges his love for her, and the necessary mutuality of any such acknowledgement. These two have earned their escape from the nightmarish cityscape in which everyone's humanity is at risk.

THE MORTALITY OF FLESH AND BLOOD

What allows Deckard to redeem his humanity is the further step in his education that occurs between the two conversations with Rachel – the lesson that Roy Baty undertakes to deliver in the film's climactic sequence in the Bradbury Building. But what licenses Roy to deliver this lesson is his own developing education about what it is to be human, and in particular his coming to learn that acquiring a more extended span of life would go no way towards achieving or establishing his own humanity.

What does it mean to claim that human beings are mortal? Perhaps that they are not immortal, that human beings do not live forever – that a human life must end at some point. This contrast encourages the view that human beings are mortal because their lives occupy a finite quantity of time, that their days are numbered and destined to run out (soon) after three-score years and ten. This is plainly the view taken by Roy Baty and his group; their dangerous return to Earth is motivated by the desire for more life – the desire to extend their allotted span of days until it matches that of a human being. One brief scene in the film disinters and undermines the misunderstandings upon which this project is predicated with dizzying speed and subtlety.

After Deckard has shot the replicant Zhora, he is accosted by her partner Leon – who observed the 'retirement' – and dragged into an alley, where Leon administers a savage beating to the blade runner. The dialogue here bears a great deal of weight:

Leon: How old am I?
Deckard: I don't know.
Leon: My birthday is April 10th, 2017. How long do I live?
Deckard: Four years.
Leon: More than you. Painful to live in fear, isn't it? Nothing
          is worse than having an itch you can't scratch.
Deckard: I agree.
Leon: Wake up – time to die.

Much of our sympathy for the replicants in this film relates to what we (and they) perceive as a deprivation: their genetically-engineered four year lifespan is far shorter than that which any human being can (barring accidents) rely upon, and it entails that they know from the first moment of their existence the precise date of their death. But Leon's interrogation of Deckard puts this assumption in question: for his ability to kill the blade runner destroys the illusion that a normal human lifespan trumps one with replicant limitations – death cannot thus be kept at a biblical arms length. Indeed, Leon here begins to emerge as a figure of real power as he names the moment of Deckard's death; it is as if his knowledge of the specific day on which he will die allows him to master and turn to his own account our common fear of dying, whereas frail human beings can never be sure when their end will come. At just this point, however, our impression of replicant superiority is in turn exploded, for Rachel saves Deckard by shooting Leon in the head – thus proving that knowing the date at which one's death is inevitable is not the same as knowing when one will die.

The moral is clear: mortal finitude is not reducible to the fact of our finite lifespan; it is rather constituted by the fact that every moment of human life is necessarily shadowed by the possibility of its own non-existence. Death is not an abstract or distant limit to life, an indeterminate but inevitable boundary to the succession of our days, but rather a presence in every moment of our existence. This is an idea Heidegger captures in his notion of human existence as Being-towards-death, where death is understood as the possibility of our own impossibility; and its emergence reveals the irrelevance of any distinction between replicants and human beings that is grounded on the length of their lifespans or the certainty with which they can predict an end to their lives on a given day. Both are alive and both possess consciousness; hence both will die, and both are conscious of that fact. Whether either will attain a grasp of its full significance is another question, but it is one that both face – which means that replicants stand in a human relationship towards death.

Roy Baty's quest for Tyrell and his ability to extend the replicant lifespan thus appears as a denial rather than an acknowledgement of mortality; but it is only through his encounter with Tyrell that this is brought home to him. For Roy's maker quickly dismisses the topic of the bio-mechanical limitations to extending replicant lifespan ('All of this is academic'), and instead introduces the two central notions this film will advance as integral to any authentic acknowledgement of human mortality, when he says 'He who burns twice as brightly burns half as long. And you have burned so very very brightly, Roy . . . Revel in your time.'

For Tyrell, the value or worth of Roy's life is determined not by its length but by the intensity with which he experiences each moment of it – in other words (and again tracing out paths followed by Heidegger), by its manifestation of a specific attitude towards the temporality of his own existence. The transience of the present moment is taken not to show its insignificance but the nature of its significance – the fact that it is a moment in transition, always having been delivered from the future and always about to be delivered over to the past, and hence that human existence is always endless becoming. All human experience is present experience or it is nothing; hence to fail to engage with the present moment is to fail to engage with one's life as such. But to engage properly with it means acknowledging that it is inextricably related to past and future; hence to live one's life authentically is to let every moment burn brightly whilst (perhaps by) still acknowledging that each such moment will pass.

Tyrell talks of this as revelling in one's time. This reference to revelry or play shows that the Nietzschean subtext of *Alien* is here re-emerging, but this time Scott is invoking Nietzsche's Zarathustra, who speaks constantly of the overman (the self-overcoming human being, the individual who understands himself as essentially transitional) as one who dances through life with lightness and grace. The Heideggerian notion of authentic Being-towards-death, of living each moment to the full whilst respecting its essential transitoriness, is here interpreted as a matter of revelling in the possibilities of act and performance that the fact of embodied, finite existence makes possible.

Roy is dimly aware of this from the outset; it is why, when Pris recites the Cartesian dictum 'I think therefore I am' in Sebastian's apartment, he responds by saying 'Very good, Pris – now show him why'. But the Nietzschean connection Tyrell forges allows him to see that the true significance or point of the moments which make up one's life should be generated from within that life rather than from a reliance upon external guarantors. For Zarathustra, the overman's authenticity was underwritten by the doctrine of eternal recurrence: one had achieved a fully human life only if, when faced with the chance to have one's life over again, one could sincerely desire that not a single moment within it should be changed. This vision is of life as a self-contained whole, its parts hanging together in utter self-sufficiency; and such a self-authenticating life could have no need for sources of value or worth external to itself.

Hence Nietzsche's association of the overman with the death of God; for the Christian God is the traditional external guarantor of the worth of human life, and in so far as His presence tempts us to refer the worth of our existence to Him, His removal from the scene becomes an essential mark of human authenticity. Nietzsche narrates this removal as the murder of God by human beings in order to underline the need to accept full responsibility for what is involved in accepting full responsibility for our lives; and by enacting this narrative – by murdering his creator in a way which brings an anguished 'Oh my God!' from Sebastian – Roy proves that he has learnt the lesson Tyrell wished to teach him. In his final encounter with Deckard, he tries to pass on that lesson.

On one level, Roy's pursuit of Deckard through the decaying Bradbury building is motivated by revenge – for the latter's execution of Pris and the other replicants.; their memory is inscribed into Deckard's body in the form of broken fingers. However, the hunt also displays Roy's overman status – specifically in his having gone beyond what Nietzsche calls the 'slave morality' of good and evil (not beyond all morality – as Ash imagines of the alien – but beyond the specifically Christian moral code which contrasts good with evil rather than with badness). Thus, Roy characterizes Deckard as the representative of good ('aren't you the good man?'), and forces him to experience 'what it is to be a slave'. The Christian imagery which collects around Roy at this point (the nail through the palm, the frieze of cruciform ventilation units on the rooftop, the dove of peace) is not something he respects but something he toys with and turns to his own purposes (as in his use of the nail to slow the advance of his own impending death); he thereby casts himself as someone whose message is at least as important for humanity as Christ's, declaring his status as the revaluator of all values.

Roy's association of slavery with living in fear, thus echoing Leon's earlier perception, also reminds us of the replicant's perception of their own status in relation to their human creators; in part, his lesson is intended to teach Deckard what he, along with all human beings, is responsible for doing to the replicants – what his denial of their humanity amounts to. But most fundamentally, it is designed to teach Deckard a lesson about his relation to death – about his mortality. Roy brings it about that Deckard feels that every moment may be his last, and Deckard's response is to flee from this threat; he functions at the level of an injured animal, incapable of anything more than an unthinking attempt to avoid the threat of extinction. His pursuer, by contrast – who knows that his own death is equally imminent, whether by genetic determinism or by Deckard's own efforts with gun and crowbar – responds to the threat by running towards it. He toys with the very threat that paralyses Deckard; he sees that, since mortality is as internal to human existence as embodiment, genuine humanity turns on finding the right relation to it.

We are thereby presented with inauthentic and authentic ways of living a human life in the face of its mortality. Deckard's flight denies the ubiquity of this threat – as if an escape from Roy would amount to an escape from the threat he incarnates. Roy treats the same threat playfully. His mourning over Pris is transformed into a mock wolf-howl, an imitation of the huntsman's pack which signals that the game of life and death is afoot; he describes firing on an unarmed man as 'not very sporting', his response to attack is to cry 'That's the spirit!', and most importantly, he declares to Deckard that 'You'd better get it up, or I'm going to have to kill you. Unless you're alive, you can't play, and if you can't play . . .'.

Like Zarathustra's disciples, Roy is dancing on the edge of the abyss, performing his version of Pris' cartwheeling enactment of her thinking, embodied existence (in Sebastian's apartment). The lightness and grace of his life finds confirmation in his ability to look at death, and the death of love, without fear or hysteria. And he wants to teach this to Deckard: if to play is to be fully alive, not to play is to be reduced to death-in-life or merely animal existence. If you can't play, you might as well be dead.

Deckard's response to death is inauthentic because it transforms his own death from an (omnipresent) possibility to an actuality: it extinguishes his humanity. So Roy teaches him the difference between possibility and actuality; he allows Deckard (and us) to spend long minutes on the edge of his existence, pushes him to the edge of a real abyss, making death seem unavoidable – and then he rescues him. And he underlines the point of that lesson by making manifest, at the moment of his own death, that he has revelled in his time.

> I've seen things you people wouldn't believe: attack-ships on fire off the shoulder of Orion; I watched c-beams glitter in the dark near the Tannhauser Gate. All those moments will be lost in time, like tears in rain. Time to die.

He has lived each moment of his life to the full without denying its transitory place in the ineluctable stream of time; and any such denial would amount to denying the essential structure of human experience as such. It would, moreover, count as a further and more profound failure of acknowledgement to wish to bequeath one's experiences and memories to others – as if one could outlive oneself, as if one's moments of consciousness were alienable, as if one's mortality could be sloughed off. Heidegger understands our relation to our own death as the clearest expression of this truth. He describes it as our ownmost, nonrelational possibility: no one can die another's death for him, just as no one can die our death for us, and that is precisely what makes our death, when it comes, our ownmost possibility. Roy's calm and moving last words manifest just this authentic understanding, and they cry out for acknowledgement as such.

It is Deckard upon whom the responsibility falls of responding to that cry. To acknowledge their significance is to acknowledge not just what they say, but the fact that they are Roy's last words – part of his last moments, a testament to his life and to life as such. Deckard blinks, as if to clear his vision, and then provides Roy with an epitaph:

> Maybe he loved life more than he ever had before. All he wanted were the same answers any of us want . . . All I could do was to sit there and watch him die.

Deckard sees not only that his tormentor's nature is precisely the same as his own, but also that the only way in which to acknowledge his human mortality at the moment of its ending is to acknowledge that Roy's death is his own – not to try hysterically to postpone it, or to try incoherently to take it upon himself, but to watch that death and watch it as the death of another human being, a human other. The authenticity of this acknowledgement shows that Deckard has learned his lesson, about acknowledging others and about acknowledging mortality. As Inspector Gaff puts it, he has done a man's job, the task of any genuine human being; and Roy's bequest to Deckard culminates in the resurrection of Rachel. It's a pity she won't live – but then again, who does?

EXCURSUS: THE DIRECTOR'S CUT

If these ideas are true to the basic tenor of *Blade Runner*'s narrative, then it must be acknowledged that the alterations to the original theatrical release version embodied in the recent 'Director's Cut' are at some distance from the deep sources of the film's power. To be sure, it is good to see the removal of the hastily-created, sunlit epilogue (in which Rachel is 'revealed' to have been given an ordinary human lifespan in order to create a happy ending which contradicts the whole thrust of the film's thoughtfulness) and of the voice-over (despite its occasional touches of wit and poetry, and its overall confirmation that Scott is here once again fusing or hybridizing the science fiction genre – this time, with that of Chandleresque *film noir*). But the sole significant addition – the restoration of a unicorn image within Deckard's reverie at the piano – has commonly been taken as intended to answer a question whose relevance to the film's central issues is itself questionable. For this inserted memory-image ensures that Gaff's placing of an origami unicorn at Deckard's apartment signifies the availability of a means of access to Deckard's memories that (just like Deckard's access to Rachel's memories) is explicable only if Deckard is himself a replicant – thus giving a literal significance to Rachel's sarcastic question about whether he has himself ever taken a V-K test. Since, however, the film itself places replicants and humans in exactly the same position with respect to its central questions (the acknowledgement of mortality and of one another), such an apparently momentous revelation about Deckard's status makes precisely no difference to the trajectory and terminus of his education. We might therefore be better advised to think of this added scene or image as itself a test of its viewers' capacity to acknowledge the film that frames it, by testing whether they recognize that it is the film's central concern to shift our conception of its importance.

ENFRAMING AND ACKNOWLEDGEMENT

It is not, then, difficult to see *Blade Runner* as a continuation of the study that Ridley Scott began in *Alien* of the flesh and blood embodiedness of human beings, and of their attempts to repress (and to overcome their repression) of its conditions and consequences. In the earlier film, this study focuses on the reproductive drive of the flesh – upon its sexuality and generativity, and upon its subordination of individual integrity and autonomy to the demands of life as such. In the later film, it focuses on the internal relationship between life and death, on the body's openness to its own mortality, and on the dependence of individual human flourishing upon acknowledging that fact, and upon one individual's acknowledgement of and by others. A certain Nietzschean vision of human existence can be seen to hold this study together, as it moves from a conception of life as rapacious and devouring will-to-power, a Moloch to which the human individual is sacrificed, to a conception of what the flourishing of a human life within such an ordering of the cosmos might look like. This same background of ideas might also account for the vestigial presence of religious, and more specifically Christian, ideas in *Alien*: for *Blade Runner* appears to declare an investment in their overcoming (and the much later *Gladiator*, with its resolutely pagan representation of a world in which human suffering is ultimately beyond redemption, might be seen as one culmination of Scott's desire to imagine a world unpolluted by essentially Christian thought).

Another constant in Scott's science fiction universe is, unsurprisingly, technology – more specifically, a deep interest in studying its impact on human forms of life. Indeed, the physical and spiritual landscape of *Blade Runner* is very similar to the microcosm of human life manifest in the *Nostromo*: the remnants of humanity left behind by the off-world settlers find themselves in a world without sunlight, and dwarfed by their own technological achievements. Like Ash, the replicants incarnate the threat of technology coming to control its creators; their presence on earth demands an extremity of hostile response, as if they instantiate a threat to the very essence of what remains of humanity. And yet that feared future, of human fusion with or absorption into the technological, is already manifest in the children of Earth – in the low hiss of wheels as a swarm of them glide by on their bikes, in the jabbering city-speak arguments they have over machinery stolen from vehicles, in the distorting layers of material wrapped around their small heads and bodies.

Heidegger would recognize this as the landscape of what he called 'the age of technology'. Such an age treats the natural world as a store of resources and raw materials for human purposes – rivers as hydroelectric power sources, forests as a standing reserve of paper, the wind as currents of potential energy – a perspective that is extended to the cosmos as a whole in Scott's vision of off-world mining and of the *Nostromo*'s general and specific purposes (to recover mineral ore from the other end of the universe, and to requisition an alien species as a weapon). Heidegger contrasted this attitude with that of acknowledging and respecting nature as a field of objects, forces and living beings each with their own specific essence or Being, to the comprehension of which the Being of human beings was uniquely attuned.

Heidegger's preferred term for the destructive grasp of nature as standing reserve is 'enframing' – a term which is likely to recall any film-maker to the fact that his own artistic medium is more dependent than any other upon technology. The material basis of film is the recording capacity of the camera – the automatic production of an image of the world exhibited before the camera, and its consequent reproduction and projection on screen.[6] Since this photographic basis of cinema seems to satisfy one of mankind's perennial fantasies – that of recording the world without the mediation of human subjectivity – it is not difficult to imagine that the technological basis of film might inherently tend towards the elimination of the human. Since, however, every film director's role is precisely to take responsibility for enframing the world, for meaning the composition and exclusion constituted by each frame in her film, her attempts to utilize the camera for artistic purposes can be seen as an attempt to find a possibility of human flourishing within the heart of the humanly threatening age of technology – to subvert that threat from within.

We might reasonably expect these issues to come to a head when the camera is directed to frame human beings. When a human being is placed before the camera, what is consequently projected on screen is plainly related to its human origin, but it is equally plainly not identical with it. A photograph of an object is not the object itself, but what we see in the photograph is surely the object photographed; certainly, it is far from easy to identify any specific respect in which the two differ (to name any feature lacked or possessed by one in comparison with the other). Hence, the question: Is the humanity of the camera's subject preserved or distorted or destroyed by its cinematic transcription or transformation? What, in short, becomes of human beings on film?

It is not difficult to see that this question is internal to *Blade Runner* – that this film in part takes the condition of film as its subject. The theme is announced in its opening sequence, in which the camera's long journey over the cityscape to the Tyrell Corporation building is intercut with close-ups of an unblinking, all-seeing eye; and an eye in which what is on screen is reflected but which is identified with no character in the world of the film can only be the eye through which the viewer sees that world – the eye of the camera and its director.

A further identification between the director of this film and Deckard is established when the blade runner is shown sitting in a darkened room observing photographs of the replicants and a recording of Leon's execution of another blade runner projected on a screen before him. It is confirmed by his use of the television set in his apartment to analyse a photograph of Zhora's apartment, when he is shown calling for close-ups and tracking shots within the photographed room (quite as if he were within the room itself). It is all-but-declared by his professional association with the Voight-Kampff machine – an obvious surrogate for the camera. And of course, what he gazes at through this machine's viewfinder are the faces of replicants – human replicas, humanlike beings whose humanness is under suspicion, to be discovered or deemed absent by the gaze of the camera.

Does this association suggest that the attentions of the camera are lethal to human subjects? Or does it rather suggest that the camera – perhaps precisely because of its refusal of human subjectivity – is as capable of confirming the humanity of those placed before it as of denying it? Since *Blade Runner* shows its surrogate director as viewing things along the barrel of his gun at least as often as through the V-K machine, we might say that it equates the camera with a death-dealing piece of technology. Even here, however, at the end, the film discriminates between what Deckard's gun can do, and what it actually does. For all his retirements of the other replicants, when he returns to Rachel in his apartment he initiates her resurrection by removing her shroud with his gun. This tells us that although the camera (like a gun) has an inherent capacity to deny humanity, it is capable of being used to acknowledge and affirm it. What matters is the manner in which it is used.

Just as, within the world of the film, the flourishing of any given person's humanity requires its acknowledgement by her others, so the flourishing of the humanity of anyone placed before the camera's gaze is determined not by its technological basis but by the use to which it is put by the director employing it. He can either transform subjects into what replicants are thought to be, simulacra of humanity; or he can actualize and preserve their subjectivity, as Deckard learns to do with Rachel. Hence, any failure of acknowledgement in a film is the director's responsibility, a failure of his own humanity; and whether or not he will succeed or fail in this respect cannot be predicted apart from an assessment of each film he makes. Even when he succeeds, however, that success can as easily be denied as acknowledged by his film's viewers – by, for example, their assuming in advance that his film is merely a generic exercise, or just another Hollywood blockbuster.

Alien is, I would say, far less interested in these questions about the nature of film than is *Blade Runner*. But it offers one internal representation of an issue that is central to any understanding of cinema as a medium, that is recognizably related to the reflexive issues addressed in *Blade Runner*, and that is powerfully determinative of the future development of the 'Alien' universe. For one aspect of the mysterious transformative powers of the camera upon human subjects is the unpredictable but ungainsayable way in which its gaze can make some actors into stars and ensure that others never attain that state – in which it allows physiognomy to become destiny. And the gradual, essentially unpredictable but obscurely satisfying emergence from the *Nostromo*'s crew of Ripley as the main human protagonist and hero of *Alien* is at once the cause and a mythical representation of Sigourney Weaver's translation (by means of the complex interaction of her as yet relatively unformed but already distinctive physiognomy with her character and its vicissitudes under the gaze of Ridley Scott's camera) into stardom. The other films in the 'Alien' series will become increasingly obsessed with giving an account of this unaccountable, precarious but undeniable phenomenon.

Aliens © 1986 20th Century-Fox Film. Reproduced by courtesy of the Roland Grant Archive.

Two

TERMINATING MATERNITY

James Cameron's first film, *Terminator*, concerns a threat posed to the future of the human race by the unintended evolution of a species of machines which responds to a threat to its own survival from its creators (who try to unplug SkyNet, the self-aware strategic defence computer who 'fathers' this species) by trying to annihilate them – first by nuclear war, then by genocide. The machines send a cybernetic organism back through time to kill the woman who will give birth to the leader of the successful human resistance; and the film charts the ensuing struggle between this 'terminator' and a resistance soldier sent by his leader to protect that woman. By the end of the film, Sarah Connor has been transformed from an under-achieving waitress and overly-trusting dater of unsuitable men to a mother capable of terminating the terminator even after her protector's death; she drives off into the desert, equipped to take on the task of preparing the child now growing in her womb for his future military role.

It is not difficult to imagine the producers of the 'Alien' series regarding this film as a calling card or show reel that might have been specifically designed to demonstrate Cameron's suitability for taking charge of their planned sequel. *Terminator* shows Cameron to be imaginatively at home in the field of science fiction, whilst being comfortable with the idea of a strong female character at the centre of this traditionally male-oriented genre; he has invented a 'villain' who represents an evolutionarily superior race whose very existence threatens the future of the human species; and he has embedded the duel between these two protagonists within a thematic structure that focuses explicitly on issues of survival and repro-duction, of sexual difference and female generativity. Moreover, *Terminator* has one distinctive and much-prized cinematic quality of which Ridley Scott's *Alien* had no particular need – a well-paced, driving narrative that links explosive and violent action scenes in a smoothly escalating sequence. Inviting Cameron to take the next step in the 'Alien' story must have seemed like bowing to the inevitable – acknowledging that director and subject-matter were made for one another, each the other's fate or destiny.

The imaginative empathy between Cameron and Scott in fact extends beyond the latter's work in *Alien* to his further investigation of distinctively human existence in *Blade Runner*. For, of course, the peculiarly powerful dread induced by *Terminator*'s eponymous villain (both in the film's characters and in its viewers) is best understood as responsive not to the fact that its distinctive nature (flesh and blood encasing a titanium alloy combat chassis) makes it uniquely capable of dealing death and of dealing with the threat of its own death, but rather to the fact that it *is* death. The terminator is death itself, embodied and made real: its mere presence spells death, it has no interest, emotion or purpose other than causing death, and it cannot itself be killed (Death cannot die). As the resistance soldier Kyle Reese puts it: 'It cannot be bargained with, it cannot be reasoned with, it doesn't feel pity or remorse or fear, and it absolutely will not stop until you are dead.'

Heidegger's characterization of death as one's ownmost, nonrelational, not-to-be-outstripped possibility might easily have been the terminator's blueprint. It is dedicated, programmed, to seek one specific individual's death; and neither the death of those who share her name (the two other Sarah Connors that the terminator kills first), nor the death of those who try to stand between her and it (the police, Reese), can prove any kind of substitute. Hence, in the end, Sarah is deprived of any helpers and friends, and proves incapable of escaping her terminator by fleeing from it, whether intellectually or physically. The comforting but inauthentic idea that one's death is a future event, something that comes gradually and predictably towards us as our lives extend themselves in time, is annihilated by the terminator's disorienting capacity to be projected into any present moment of our lives; and once it is so projected, once its gaze fixes on its target, it cannot be outstripped by driving, running or crawling away from it. Sarah has to confront her terminator on her own – face to face with the titanium death's head, stripped of its human guise, through the bars of the robotic metal-press. (And Cameron's sequel to his own first film will have much to say about whether her crushing of the terminator in that press should be understood as her overcoming her own death, or rather as its coming to inhabit her life, and the life of the human species as such.)

In this respect, of course, Sarah Connor is no different from any other human being: if the terminator only represented death, or human mortality as such, then we would each have our own terminator, capable of appearing at any moment of our lives to isolate us from our relatives and friends and confront us with the essential non-necessity of our individual existence. But Sarah Connor is targeted by her terminator for a more specific reason, one which picks her out as a woman, and as a particular woman: she is to be terminated because she is to give birth to the human male who will bring about the extermination of the machines, and hence ensure the survival of the human race. In other words, her death is a kind of advance (or is it retrospective?) abortion; and it is required because her generativity as a female stands for the generativity of the human species as such. Her capacity to become a mother symbolizes the human capacity to reproduce itself, our possession of a future.

There is a clear sense, then, in which Sarah Connor is meant to exemplify an affirmative and empowering vision of femaleness. She is exemplary of humanity as such, and her generativity is what will keep human history open to the future; and although her reception of this knowledge is at first panic-stricken, the film charts a real growth in her character towards a kind of self-sufficiency − for in acquiring a repertoire of defensive and offensive techniques (both physical and psychological), she acquires the strength to take on the terminator by herself, and to take on her responsibilities to her future son and the human race as such. In this respect, *Terminator* observes the creation of a female warrior.

On the other hand, however, what picks Sarah out as the vital figure in this narrative is also what sidelines her as an individual. For, of course, in so far as her worth to the human race turns entirely on the man to whom she will give birth, it turns on her offspring rather than herself − and on a male child, at that. This underlying sense that her femaleness is valuable only instrumentally, as a means to reproducing maleness, is reinforced by the displacements of causality that the film's disruption of the temporal order makes possible. For it turns out that Sarah acquires Reese (and hence not only self-protection, but the education for survival and motherhood that he imparts) only because he was sent to her by the resistance leader to whom she will give birth, her son John; and since it further emerges that Reese is the destined father of her son, the film ends by conferring on John Connor the power to authorize his own birth. Not only does he provide what is required for his mother to survive long enough to give birth to him, he also chooses (and brings his mother together with) the man who will be his father. Indeed, since their conjunction brings about not only his conception but his mother's acquisition of the beliefs and skills necessary to bring him up so as to become the hero of humanity, we can say that John Connor is the author not only of his own family (the [re]birth of Sarah and Kyle as warrior-mother and warrior-father) and his own birth, but of every aspect of his life, and hence of himself.

Within this bizarre displacement of the familiar human family structure, Sarah Connor comes to seem more and more like a counter or token in a complex relationship between men. For whilst John Connor's foreknowledge of the past is what allows him to give Kyle Reese the mission that will make him his father, from Kyle's point of view that same mission allows him to write himself into his hero's own history. He is enabled to become the father of the man he most adores in the human race's post-nuclear future; he thereby finds at once a displaced heterosexual mode of expression for his love for humanity's ultimate warrior, and a means of ensuring that the son he fathers will be exactly the son he could have wished – thus insulating paternity from its inherent openness to the contribution of female fertility and of unpredictable events, from its openness to contingency, and the loss of control that such openness entails.

Of course, Sarah's room for independent manoeuvre within this exchange between men is not entirely eliminated. She is the one who refuses to accept Kyle's (admittedly half-hearted) attempts to disown his declaration of love for her, and thus brings about the sexual intercourse through which John Connor is conceived; and within that declaration, Kyle is insistent that he fell in love with Sarah primarily because of the expression on her face in a photograph of her. Kyle thereby seeks to present the narrative of *Terminator* as a love story, a quest across time motivated by love at first sight, and hence by the woman who elicited that love. On the other hand, he is given his first sight of Sarah in that photograph, and hence Sarah herself, by John; and the final scene of the film reveals that the photograph captures her expression just as she is thinking of Kyle himself, and of their one night of love. In other words, he sees the consummation of their love in her eyes, and hence sees himself as already beloved by her (and thereby sees the removal of any risk in his declaring his love – the removal of the possibility of refusal or non-reciprocation, and hence the removal of Sarah's autonomy, her otherness); and he also sees his beloved son, already alive within her. In short, what he sees in this photograph is not primarily Sarah but himself and his offspring; he sees in her the consummation of a narcissistic fantasy of male sexual potency, of paternity and patriarchal family structure.

This sense that Sarah's photograph is not so much a love token as an expression of her tokenistic role in a relationship between men is confirmed by its place in one of the most disorienting sequences of the film, in which Sarah – hiding beneath a bridge with Kyle, just after his diagnosis as paranoid has been disproved by the terminator's destruction of the police station, and just before their lovemaking – appears to dream of a future in which Kyle is killed by an infiltrating terminator. In fact, since the dream is initiated and sustained by Kyle's description of his previous life in the future, it would be more accurate to say that Sarah realizes her future lover's words, uncovering a certain range of meaning in them. And what she realizes is a vision of his death, which occurs just after he has been poring over her photograph, and which results in that photo being consumed by flames before his dying eyes. Kyle's death at such a point in the future – that is, before his return to Sarah's time – would amount to the death of John Connor's father, and hence to John himself never being born. This is a salutary reminder of Kyle's own significance in the film's story beyond that of protector and educator; but the sequence also declares that his removal from the narrative would mean that Sarah would never be reborn as John's mother, hence never be in a position to be photographed whilst thinking of her dead lover and his unborn child. The destruction of that photograph thus signals that her primary role is as Kyle's lover and John's mother; her significance goes up in flames when their existence is consumed by a terminator's lethal attentions.

It is worth noting that the spatially, temporally and emotionally displaced family structure of which this photograph is the currency is not entirely unfamiliar. Its most obvious cultural precedent lies at the heart of Christianity, in the Holy Family. There, too, we have a single male offspring, whose impending birth is announced by a guardian angel, whose initials are J.C. and whose destiny is to be the saviour of the human race; and given that this child's divinity participates in the trinitarian structure of the Christian God, we can say that he, too, creates his own family and authors his own birth. True, Cameron's (post- or perhaps pre-) nuclear family displaces the sign of virginity from the mother to the father of this family (Kyle's declaration of love embodies a declaration of his own previous celibacy); but even this may rather indicate that Kyle, as the merely surrogate father of this family, in this respect resembles the Holy Family's surrogate father, Joseph. Otherwise, however, Cameron's representation of Sarah as the family's mother seems quite strikingly to reproduce the combination of apparent centrality but ultimate marginality typically thought to define the place of Mary (and hence, femaleness) in Christianity – the woman as temporary host, vehicle or medium for a creative transaction between or within an essentially male principle of cosmic divinity. (Here is yet another point of contact with the logic of *Alien*, as well as a pointer towards a deeply buried religious dimension in that film.)

We should not, however, overlook the fact that the photograph of Sarah – by its very nature – reminds us that the material basis of the medium of film is photographic, and hence that one range of its significance in *Terminator* might be to act as the vehicle of Cameron's reflections upon the nature of the medium in which he is beginning to work. Several lines of thought find their origins here. First, if the photograph of Sarah is a synecdoche of the film in which it appears, and which is in part constituted by sequences of such photographs, then the person who is ultimately responsible for it – for its framing and composition, and for its appearance as a symbol of the medium of film – is the film's director.

This is confirmed by the fact that the photograph is taken for, preserved and handed on to its most avid viewer by a character whose initials are J.C. – a character who is never seen in the film, but is presented by it as the ultimate author of the events it depicts. Indeed, just as this film records John Connor's authorization of his own birth, so we might think of the film itself as James Cameron's creation of himself as a film director, at this point someone for whom this film constitutes his entire body (of serious work). And if this interpretation (with its equation of the film's director with a character whom the film further equates with God) implies a certain hubris in Cameron, it is as well to recall that this photograph of Sarah is envisaged as having more than one future. In one, it makes possible the reality that the photograph itself depicts, and amounts to a certain kind of redemption – a re-achievement of genuine humanity, say, in a medium that is otherwise reduced to the merely commercial; in another (that of dream or nightmare), it is consumed by flames, its very existence aborted by an unforeseeable evolution of time and more particularly of the very technology without which it would not even have been conceivable as a cinematic work of art. One might even think of this dream as showing Cameron's prophetic awareness of the fundamental importance that technological advances in the medium of cinema will have in the evolution and evaluation of his future career as a director.

A second line of thought opens up from the fact that this photograph finds itself central to a dream sequence in which the film's necessary distortions of time and space find their deepest and darkest expression. Such distortions are, of course, commonplace in the genre of science fiction – the natural home of time travel; but is there any reason to think, as this film's placement of its central symbol for itself suggests, that this familiar generic resource taps into something internal to the nature of the cinematic medium itself?

Here, we return to an ontological question we encountered in the previous chapter of this book: what exactly is the difference between an object in a photograph and the object itself? Stanley Cavell has argued that a photograph of an object is not, as a painting of it may be, a visual representation of that object (it does not stand for that object, nor form a likeness of it), but rather a visual transcription of it.[1] However, it does not transcribe the sight or look or appearance of an object in the way in which a recording can be said to transcribe the sound of an object – primarily because a sight is either an extra-ordinary happening or an object itself (the aurora borealis or the Grand Canyon); what we see when we sight something is not the sight of an object but the object itself. Objects can be said to have or to make sounds, but not to have or to make sights; so there is nothing of the right sort for a photograph to be a photograph of short of the object itself. And yet, a photograph of Linda Hamilton is not Linda Hamilton in the flesh.

Cavell's mode of resolving this apparent paradox is to suggest that we are approaching the question of this undeniable difference with a questionable assumption – that the objects in a photograph or film must differ in some specifiable respect from real objects, one having or lacking a feature that the other does not. We can distinguish real objects from one another by specifying criteria, determining specific differences between them; and we can distinguish between objects in a photograph or film using the same criteria. But we cannot distinguish real objects from objects in a photograph in such a way; there are no criteria which distinguish a photographed object from the object itself – no specific respect (eye colour? height? running style?) in which Linda Hamilton in a photograph or film differs from Linda Hamilton in the flesh. This does not mean we cannot distinguish between them; it means that the distinction must be specified not in terms of visible differences but in terms of the different relationships in which we stand to them.

A useful comparison here is our relationship to the characters in a play: according to Cavell, those characters do not differ in any specifiable respect from our fellow human beings outside the theatre, but our relationship to them differs. More precisely, whilst we can place ourselves in the same time as the play's characters (can confront each presented moment of the play's events as the present moment of its character's lives, importing neither our knowledge of its ending nor any assumption that what has already happened dictates their fate), we and they cannot occupy the same space (there is no path from our position to theirs, we are not in their presence). By contrast, the viewers of a photograph or film share neither a space nor a time with the object or person photographed; they are not in its physical presence, and the moment at which the object was captured by the camera is not made present to them and cannot be made present by them (our absence is mechanically assured, not something for which we are responsible). In short, the world of a photograph does not (and cannot) exist *now*.

> The reality in a photograph is present to me while I am not present to it; and a world I know, and see, but to which I am nevertheless not present (through no fault of my subjectivity) is a world past. In viewing a movie . . . I am present not at something happening, which I must confirm, but at something that has happened, which I must absorb (like a memory). In this movies resemble novels, a fact mirrored in the sound of narration itself, whose tense is the past.
>
> (Cavell, *The World Viewed*, Cam., Mass.: Harvard University Press, 1971, pp. 23, 25–6)

If this is right, then there might appear to be a conflict between the genre of science fiction, with its projections of future social and technological arrangements, and the grain of

the film medium. For is there not something temporally dis-
ordered and disorienting about being present at the projection
of a narrative of something that has happened, when that story
– being set in the future – is presented as not yet having
happened? Would that not make the experience of viewing
such films one of absorbing a memory of what is to come –
and what might that be like?

In *Terminator*, this is the basic shape of the experience of both
of its central human protagonists. Everything that Kyle tells
Sarah is of her, his and the human future, but he describes it
from memory; his key message to her from her as yet unborn
son is one that he explicitly says he had to memorize, and the
photograph of her that motivates his every action records a
moment in her life that is yet to occur. For Sarah, when that
photograph is taken and given to her, its subjects – herself, her
love for Kyle and her son – immediately move into the past;
but she then drives into a future whose lineaments are dictated
by her memory of Kyle's and her son's memories, as embodied
in that photograph. In this respect, Cameron's placing of
the photograph of Sarah at the heart of his narrative's most
intense displacements of space and time signifies his awareness
of the fact that the film he is directing is investigating (through
the time travel narrative that creates and trades upon those
displacements) a fundamental condition of the possibility of
films about the future.

Sarah's condition as a character thus resembles our condition as viewers: like her, we see the future only through Kyle's
memories of it, whether privately visualized (as in the wrecked
car before he finds Sarah) or as described to her. Hence, like
us, she is presented with, and feels compelled to inhabit, a
future that is fixed or determined in the manner of the past,
as if remembering her future. And what remains of the future

if it is stripped of its unknownness, its openness? What damage is thereby done to our sense of ourselves as having a future, and as having some control over what that future will be like? What happens to our individuality and freedom? And what happens to the world? The film's concluding image of the impending nuclear apocalypse does not encourage optimism.

One concluding line of thought extending from the photograph should be noted. For of course, it is a photograph of Sarah Connor at her moment of rebirth as the warrior mother of a warrior son, which is to say it is a photograph of Linda Hamilton at the moment of her possible birth as a star. How will the peculiar conjunction of physiognomy, character and director determine the trajectory of her cinematic transfiguration? James Cameron will return to this.

REITERATING FAMILY VALUES: REAL AND IDEAL

If we think of *Alien* as an entity whose identity was determined by the dovetailing contributions of a specific director and a specific scenario or script – the two wrapping or warping around one another to form the double helix of its internal code or programme – then *Aliens* is what results when one helical strand from the original entity is combined with another from the director-scenario double helix of *Terminator*. The analogy limps, of course; but its emphasis upon the combination and recombination of sequences of coding goes some way towards capturing what is distinctive about Cameron's approach to the delicate and burdensome responsibility of writing and directing a sequel to a critically acclaimed (if not commercially lucrative) film with a highly specific style and subject matter. For in essence, Cameron constitutes *Aliens* from displaced re-presentations of the basic elements from which *Alien* is itself constructed.

The depth and degree of this repetition are as difficult to measure as they are to credit, because of the multiplicity of levels at which the repetition occurs. At the level of basic plot structure, we see Cameron restage the crew's reawakening from hypersleep to face the alien nightmare, their trip from a mothership by shuttle to the planet of the alien wreck, their gradual elimination by their enemy, the climactic need for the nuclear destruction of a human technological edifice infested by the alien species, and of course the double-climax structure of which Cameron also made use in *Terminator*. Re-enactment is also the dominant principle at the level of individual scenes – for example, the panic-stricken strategy and weapons-evaluation meeting after the first alien incursion, complete with disparaging references to the android's inadequate contribution to their cause; Ripley's encounter with a facehugger in the medical lab facilities, complete with her falling backwards to throw it off whilst armed men throw themselves across her; and the scene (restored in its entirety in the Director's Cut) in which Scott's leisurely prowling of the corridors and crevices of the *Nostromo* before the crew's rebirth is recapitulated (right down to pans across corridor intersections, dipping mechanical toys and empty helmets) by Cameron as our introduction to the crew of the *Sulaco*. And at the level of specific images or tableaux, beyond that of the various phases of the alien itself, we are presented with the same design of weaponry and related technology (flame guns, motion trackers, TV monitors), the same tangles of clanking chains (transposed from Brett's death scene to the Marines' birth scene), the same chaos of red lights, grilles and tunnels in the first climax, and the same second-climax vision of the last alien spiralling out into space through an airlock door. Cameron underlines this aspect of his strategy by scattering his film with the figure '2': it is stencilled on Newt's bed in the medical lab, the second drop-ship, the second elevator from the alien nest, and the airlock from which the alien queen is eventually ejected – and it might as well be stencilled on Bishop's forehead, although in fact he has to make do instead with a surname beginning with the second letter of the alphabet, following on from Ash's initial 'A'. Why does this overwhelming repetitiveness not dilute the film's undeniable pleasures, or loosen the increasing firmness of its narrative grip on us, but rather help to intensify both? In part, of course, because such repetitions provide the fundamental pleasure of recognition, allowing us to recall the pleasure those elements gave us on their first appearance, and reassuring us of the depth of our new director's familiarity with and respect for the film, and its world, that they helped constitute. More importantly, however, they give pleasure because they are not simply repetitions: for Cameron subjects his reiterated elements to various kinds of displacement or transformation.

The most obvious variation is one of magnified scale: the nuclear explosion is bigger, the weaponry and firefights more spectacular, the second climax confronts Ripley with a far more frightening variant of the alien, and accordingly provides her with a far more substantial exoskeleton than her original spacesuit (the cargo-loader). Less obviously, Cameron can utilize repetition to encourage certain expectations determined by the first film in order to subvert or invert them: this is clearest in the case of Bishop, who is made to re-enact Ash's admiring dissections of the facehugger before turning out to be Ripley's saviour – an inversion Cameron underlines by having him reduced to a dismembered state akin to Ash's final appearance for his climactic rescue of Newt.

Cameron himself refers to this aspect of his work as taking

seriously his audience's programming – not denying but acknowledging their familiarity with the first film, and their knowledge that what they are watching is a sequel to it, hence ineluctably indebted to it, the same again, but different.[2] But he encodes a further explanation of his technique of displaced repetition within the film itself – an explanation prepared for by the fact that the opening act of *Aliens* (from Ripley's rescue to her acceptance of a role in the Marine mission) presents her as someone who must relive a nightmare if she is to overcome its traumatic effects on her life. Ripley's first apparently conscious moments, which culminate in her being revealed as another victim of the alien chestburster, turn out to be a nightmare – one which she relives every night until the Company's offer of an advisory role in an expedition to annihilate the alien species gives her a chance to (as Burke puts it) get back on the horse. Hence, the first scene on board the *Sulaco* is presented pretty much exactly as was the opening sequence of *Alien*, and Cameron's multilevel reiterations of that film move into top gear, until his duplicate double-climax is resolved by a repetition of Ripley's prior ejection of the alien from her mothership. Only then can she reassure Newt that they may both dream again: only by therapeutically recalling and re-experiencing her initial traumatic encounter can she locate and disable its source.

This is, in fact, the key respect in which *Aliens* differs from its cinematic source: it takes us back to the geographical (if not the cosmic) source of the alien species, and it introduces us to two aspects of its reproductive cycle about which *Alien* is silent, but without which the alien species as such could not survive (the cocooning of living human hosts in preparation for impregnation,[3] and the mode or variant of alien life from which the eggs containing the impregnating facehuggers themselves come) – that is, it uncovers the biological as well as the geographical source of the alien species. And by forcing Ripley to confront what she is trying to repress, and thereby forcing the 'Alien' series to confront what it has so far repressed about its eponymous protagonist, Cameron presents himself as engaged in an essentially therapeutic endeavour – one in which the reiteration of that which has been repressed will bring release or liberation. It is as if Cameron takes his own film as the necessary therapy of which his predecessor's central human character and the cinematic world in which she is introduced both stand in need. He proposes, in short, to heal both Ripley and the alien narrative universe, to cure them of that which ails them; and it is in his understanding of what this requires that Cameron makes manifest his deepest acknowledgement, and his most radical subversion, of the underlying logic of Scott's prior film. For, of course, what Ripley achieves by the end of *Aliens* – her reward for confronting her deepest fears – is a family: Corporal Hicks becomes her husband, and Newt their child. Hicks has been demonstrating his fitness for this role throughout the movie; he combines quick thinking, courage, coolness under fire and a refusal to participate in the boastful, point-scoring emptiness of his fellow-soldiers' utterances with an instinctive and unflagging concern for the film's representative of childhood (he prevents Drake from shooting Newt accidentally when she is first spotted, and he is Ripley's best supporter as she tries to recover Newt from the bowels of the alien nest). Hicks is, however, more than just a suitable partner for Ripley: he is her other, the one who is prepared to have her words put in his mouth ('we'll nuke the planet from orbit – it's the only way') and hence to give her once again a voice in her own history, the sole masculine character in the movie who is represented as developing (out of the highly macho Marine culture, with its talk of taking colonists' virginity and its combination of pornography with weaponry[4]) towards the 'nurturing warrior' ideal (an ideal that the actor, Michael Biehn, also represented in *Terminator*, as Kyle Reese) – the same ideal towards which Ripley is also moving from her side of the divide of sexual difference. It is no accident that their marriage is sealed (when he gives her a wristband location tracker, which he rather too insistently tells her 'doesn't mean we're engaged or anything') just before educating her in the complexities of Marine weapons technology. Both can overcome their anxieties in battle, both do the right thing at the right time for the right reasons, both can handle themselves without losing touch with their humanity. Their union thus represents a fusion of what is deemed best in the prevailing cultural stereotypes of masculinity and femininity – the film's answer to the question implicit in the exchange between Hudson and Vasquez on the *Sulaco*: 'Have you ever been mistaken for a man?' 'No – have you?'

Ripley's understanding of the significance of Hicks' gift of the location tracker is made clear when in the scene immediately following her 'engagement' she gives the tracker to Newt, as if binding her into the union. Her accelerating inhabitation of the role of mother to Newt is, however, central to the film's development throughout: she goes after Newt in the ducts and walkways, cleans her up, defends her in the med lab against the facehuggers, promises never to leave her and fulfils that promise against all the odds. As a consequence, when Newt welcomes her back after her climactic confrontation with the alien queen, her sigh of 'Mommy!' can seem not only deeply satisfying but also disquietingly tardy – as if Newt's expectations of anyone wishing to become her mother are savagely demanding, as if motherhood itself asks for devotion beyond any rational limit. Certainly, on the film's view of the matter, if the true warrior is nurturing, the true nurturer is a warrior: it is, after all, Ripley's devotion to her daughter that generates the film's two most thrilling images of her as a soldier – when she is arming herself in the elevator going back into the alien nest, and when she walks out in the cargo loader to confront the alien queen (and deliver the film's most famous line: 'Get away from her, you bitch!').

To conceive of Ripley's overcoming of her nightmare, her healing, as the acquisition of a family shows how deeply Cameron is attuned to the logic of sexual difference and generativity implicit in *Alien*, and to Ripley's own place within that logic – fated to heroism by virtue of her obdurate refusal of heterosexual intercourse and its reproductive consequences. But the kind of family she acquires, or more precisely the way in which she acquires it, shows that Cameron's conception of what it would be for Ripley to be healed is in fact a continuation of – essentially in complicity with – the very attitude to sexuality that locks her into her nightmare. For Ripley's family has a non-biological origin: her union with her husband is not physically consummated, and she becomes a mother to Newt without conceiving, being pregnant with or giving birth to her. In short, whilst Ripley's achievement of this film's conception of female fulfilment demands that she lay her body on the line for Hicks and Newt, it allows her to avoid any acknowledgement of her body's fertility.[5]

But that which is repressed is not annihilated – indeed it has a habit of returning in an only apparently unfamiliar guise; and we know from the first film in the series where to look for the displaced expression of this vision of flesh and blood fertility as monstrous – the alien species. To be sure, Cameron's way of representing the horror of the aliens differs significantly

73 **Making Babies**

from that of Scott: without depriving himself of the specific modes of disgust aroused by its facehugging and chestbursting forms, he emphasizes two other aspects of its form of life.

The first (as the plural form of the film title suggests) is its multiplicity: the humans in this film face not a single alien being but hundreds of them. This has the cinematic advantage of enhanced scale for the fight sequences, and underlines their unstoppable reproductive drive; but it has the further consequence of allowing Cameron to represent the alien species exclusively in large numbers, and thereby to emphasize his sense of that species as itself a kind of monstrous whole, an agglomeration or incorporation of its individual members. This comes through most clearly when Hicks looks up into the overhead ducts of their last redoubt, and sees a multi-limbed, hydra-headed tangle of alien flesh apparently dragging itself through the confined space towards them. What Cameron portrays as monstrous here is not exactly community as such, but one mode of it. For the Marines represent a human mode of communal existence whose individual members are trained to subordinate themselves to the good of the whole; but their humanity is manifested in the film as their capacity to make decisions and to establish individual loyalties for themselves, in opposition to those deemed to represent the good of the community (as when Hicks and Vasquez conceal ammunition on their first foray into the alien nest, or when Vasquez and Gorman decide to sacrifice themselves in the airducts). The aliens, by contrast (like ants), have no genuinely individual existence in their community – they are foetuses or nurses or warriors, utterly subsumed by their roles within the community that is their species. They have no interests of their own, no conception of what such expressions of individuality might be; in this respect, they are monstrous.

The other new aspect of their monstrosity resides in their queen. Ripley first confronts her when, having rescued Newt from cocoonment and imminent impregnation, the pair stumble into the heart of the nest – its nursery. The camera relays to us Ripley's horrified gaze as it moves from the ranks of alien eggs, to the arrival of a new egg from a large, trembling orifice, and then back along the enormous, semi-translucent, sagging egg sac to its point of connection with the alien queen, who is revealed from tail to ornate head, her crown internal to her own cranial anatomy. The monstrosity of that egg sac – supported by resinous stays fixed to the ceiling, half-hidden by steam arising from the warm, newly-laid eggs, half-full of a soupy, slightly-bubbling liquid (as if it represented the birth of life itself from a primeval, amniotic fluid) – is so extreme that it even undercuts the awesomeness of the queen's body. It is the absolute embodiment of Ripley's vision of flesh and fertility, of the biological realm, of life as such: it is everything that she and her family are not.

And yet, of course, the queen as mother is also a mirror image of Ripley herself, as she has been transformed by Cameron's therapy – as Cameron implied even in the prologue to his film, when he introduces us to Ripley in her new apartment on Earth by focusing first on her hand as it holds a cigarette, a hand whose fingers look remarkably like the digits of the alien facehugger; and as he further suggests by presenting Ripley with a shorter haircut, the better to reveal her distinctive high cheekbones and slightly jutting jaw, so strikingly reminiscent of the sculptured alien face (physiognomy as cinematic destiny). Both are, in essence, nurturing warriors. The queen simply incarnates the reproductive drive that is internal to any species, including the human; and her aggressive impulses are as informed by her maternity as are

Ripley's – as her willingness to accept Ripley's wordless bargain ('Let us go and I won't torch your nursery') underlines. Thus far, she responds exactly as her nature demands – her motivations are as natural as they could be, and hence the monstrosity of her representation can be understood only on the assumption that nature itself (as incarnated in her) is felt to be monstrous. What transforms her from a brooding mother to a warrior is not some malevolent or gratuitous desire to destroy human beings, but rather Ripley's attack on her nursery; the queen's final pursuit of the human mother and child is driven by a desire for vengeance upon the one who slew her offspring.

This simply confirms the implicit equivalence between Ripley and the queen – since it was the same drive to protect her child that brought Ripley into the nursery in the first place. But it also suggests a certain asymmetry between the two warrior mothers – and one rather to Ripley's detriment; for it is Ripley herself who violates her implicit bargain with the queen, and thereby risks her own life and that of her child, in order to annihilate the queen's offspring. In other words, she prefers to break her word, deny her own drive for survival and reproduction and enact genocide (against a race whose predation upon her own is merely natural, and against a queen who has hitherto shown a willingness at least to accept a temporary *modus vivendi* with the human species, and hence an almost human concern for morality and children) rather than live a moment longer with the knowledge that such an incarnation of biological fertility might exist. Which of these females, we might well think, is the real bitch?

We might also recall Ripley's (self-)righteous denunciation of Burke's plan to smuggle an alien back to earth, when she says that she doesn't know which species is the worst: 'at least you don't see them fucking one another over for a percentage'. One might defend her against her own criticism by saying that her deal is not for personal gain, and that it was brokered between species rather than within one; but genocide is hardly more morally appetizing than murder, and it is hardly rendered more comprehensible when attempted in a context in which it threatens immense personal loss. In reality, what offends Ripley about Burke is what offends her about the aliens: just as the queen incarnates the threat of biological fertility, so Burke's smuggling plan both literally and symbolically threatened Ripley with the consequences of being 'fucked': Burke intended to impregnate her (and Newt) with an alien foetus in order to smuggle them past quarantine checks on Earth. Here is the deepest reason for Burke's taking on the symbolic role of Ash in the first film (with its transposition of the threat of masculine sexual violence from the realm of science to that of economics); his behaviour re-enacts Ash's attempts to kill Ripley by forcing something down her throat (and that act's denial of her voice reappears in the sequel when Burke traps Ripley in the soundproof med lab, rendering mute her appeals for help against the facehuggers). Here also is the deepest appeal of her relationship with Hicks: for their union coincides with their mutual convergence upon an essentially asexual human ideal – as if each reflects the other primarily in their transcendence of any biological sexual difference, as if the erasure of the very idea of such difference is the condition of their mutual attraction.

If further confirmation were needed of Cameron's inability to distance himself from Ripley's nightmare vision – the downside of his (and our) deep identification with her fusion of the soldier and the nurturer – it is to be found in the political significance of her genocidal impulse. Like its predecessor,

Aliens is a generic hybrid: it fuses the logic and conventions of the horror film with that of the war movie, and Cameron has more than once acknowledged that he conceived the Marine mission to LV 426 as a study of the Vietnam war – in which, on his analysis, a high-tech army confident of victory over a supposedly more primitive civilization found itself mired in a humiliating series of defeats that added up to an unwinnable war. To be sure, this analysis allows Cameron to criticize certain aspects of American culture – its adoration of the technological, its ignorance of alien cultures, its over-weening arrogance. At the same time, however, the generic background of his film, together with its specific inheritance of the alien narrative universe, ensures that the structure of his criticism works only by placing the Vietnamese in the position of absolute, and absolutely monstrous, aliens; and it rewrites the conflict it claims to analyse by allowing the Marines to win the war by destroying the planet in a nuclear explosion. It thereby supports the vision of American political hubris and xenophobia that it claims to criticize, and underwrites Ripley's genocidal impulse, the deepest expression of her repression of her human flesh and blood – both her own, and that of her offspring and her species. It appears, then, that the person most in need of healing here is the would-be therapist.

EXCURSUS: *THE ABYSS*

Whether or not as a result of perceiving this, James Cameron's next excursion into the science fiction field contains some evidence of a transformation in his attitudes to the aspects of human life so resolutely detested by Ripley. For in *The Abyss*, the lives and the marriage of its two central characters are saved by their capacity to let themselves die in the hope of rebirth. The woman goes first, as if educating her husband.

When both are trapped too many metres from their under-water mothership with only one oxygen mask between them, she chooses to allow herself to drown; her hope is that the resulting hypothermia will preserve her vital functions during the time it takes her husband to carry her back to the ship, and that hope is realized. As if empowered by her example, her husband then agrees to utilize an entirely new, SEAL-designed, breathing apparatus, intended to allow divers to operate at extreme depths; it works by filling its user's lungs with oxygen-rich fluid – hence, her husband must, in effect, allow himself to drown in order to live at the depths to which he must go in order to avert the destruction of an extraterrestrial species they have encountered. As one of the SEALs points out as a kind of reassurance, 'everyone breathes like this for nine months; your body will remember': in other words, to employ this apparatus is to return oneself to the womb. It is as powerful and beautiful an image of what is involved in human self-overcoming as one could desire; and its force in this context is redoubled by the fact that its cinematic projection required James Cameron to subordinate his best resources as a director to giving life to that SEAL's invocation of the life-giving powers of the human body, and its memory of existence between conception and birth – when it survives and flourishes only in parasitic dependence on human femininity.

ON SELF-TERMINATION

Cameron's attitude to the making of sequels, as established with *Aliens*, is re-enacted in his next exercise in the science fiction genre – *Terminator 2: Judgment Day*, the sequel to his own first film. The same implausibly pervasive repetitions of basic plot structure, specific scenes and particular seams of imagery are evident – ranging from a reiteration of the first film's chase structure and its culmination in a double climax pivoting on the death-dealing terminator's capacity to overcome even the dismemberment of his body, to Cameron's magnification of a toy lorry (crushed under the wheels of the terminator's car at the beginning of the first film) into an enormous, fully-functioning truck of exactly the same appearance hijacked by the new terminator to hunt down John Connor in the sequel's opening chase sequence. Equally predictably, however, these massive reiterations are blended with equally insistent patterns of displacement and transformation, the whole hanging together with almost algorithmic precision, and turning ultimately on Cameron's introduction of a second (kind of) terminator into his second 'Terminator' film.

In his sequel, the machines send back a prototype T-1000 (made of mimetic polyalloy, a liquid metal that can imitate anything of similar volume that it samples by physical contact), and target it on John himself rather than his mother. This single move determines every other displacement of the key characters from the first movie within the matrix of roles that film established: it allows Arnold Schwarzenegger to appear in the Kyle Reese role, as another instance of the older model of terminator he played in the first film, but now programmed by the resistance to combat the T-1000; this allows Sarah Connor to appear as a kind of human terminator, dispensing the opposite of love to her son, intending to kill the future inventor of the SkyNet technology, and seeing herself and her world as already post-nuclear; and this in turn allows John Connor himself, displaced from the unseen future, to concern himself again with the (re)construction of his own family.

This last displacement in many ways simply reiterates the bizarre family structure at the heart of Terminator, despite the fact that it prevents him from authoring his own birth in any literal sense; for once again, we find not only that John Connor is the prime mover of the plan to save his own mother, but that he in effect brings her together with a new or surrogate father – the re-programmed terminator. As Sarah herself puts it: 'It would always be there, and it would die to protect him. Of all the would-be fathers who came and went, only this machine measured up; in an insane world, it was the sane choice.'

That testimony appears to underline the very repression of the flesh and of sexual difference that we noted in *Aliens*; it identifies true fatherhood with an absence of flesh and blood, and invokes an idea of a family forged in the absence of sexual intercourse. To be sure, Sarah has given birth in the usual way to her son, but her sense of her own motherly relation to him is one in which he is not so much her own flesh and blood as everyone's, the embodiment of humanity's hope for a future: when he acts on his sense of his own particular connection to her, ordering the terminator to help him get her out of the mental hospital despite the risk of encountering the T-1000, because she is his mother, Sarah's response is to deny that connection; she tells him to protect himself, even when her interests are threatened, because his destiny as the saviour of the race is more important.

On the other hand, the film also makes clear that the person who utters those words about the perfect family is herself in a far from perfect state; it does not endorse but rather contextualizes and diagnoses their import. Education and change are at the heart of this film in a number of ways – as we see in the terminator's education in the ways of human beings, most specifically in its learning to achieve its goals without killing, and in Dyson's coming to learn and take responsibility for what he has not yet done; but its key instance of self-overcoming is that of Sarah Connor herself.

At the end of the first film, we see her on the verge of transforming herself into a warrior's mother; the second film begins by displaying the results of that self-transformation. The Sarah Connor who later finds herself trying to assassinate a fellow human being for something he has not (yet) done is someone who believes (and lives out the belief) that a warrior's mother must be all warrior and no mother – a non-nurturing soldier. In the service of the goal of preparing her son for his destiny as saviour of the human race in the war against the machines, she has become a killing machine herself. And Cameron's understanding of the source of her incarnation of deathliness is striking: it is her foreknowledge of the future.

The film's study of Sarah opens with her unsuccessful attempt to convince her psychiatrist that she has changed; but the videotaped interview in which she gives expression to her true feelings focuses on her Cassandra-like foretelling of the nuclear war of which Kyle Reese spoke, and on the impact of that knowledge of impending apocalypse upon her own sense of the world. Its impact, in short, is that she perceives herself, her fellow human beings and their world as already dead. 'You think you're safe and alive; but you're already dead. Everything is gone – you're living in a dream. Because I know what happens – it happens.' For Sarah, her knowledge of what will happen collapses the future into the past, and thereby destroys the present; because for her the future is fixed, no longer open to determination in at least some degree by the thoughts and actions of those presently alive, those thoughts and actions lose any human significance, and the significance of the lives that they go to make up also vanishes in the face of the utter loss of human significance that future nuclear war represents. She dreams of that war as annihilating children because it annihilates the future, and the primary symbol of the future in the present (the primary locus of the human sense of humanity as having a future, and of the human sense of the future as open and meaningful) is the child. In short, to know that the world will end is itself the end of the world; what Sarah knows spells the death of her world, and of herself in it – she is already dead too, and she knows it. Hence, her presence in that world can only spell death for those she encounters – not only for her son, who finds that his mother does not exist for him, but for anyone who opposes her (for what can it matter if she kills someone who is already dead?)

Three things serve to rescue Sarah from the most extreme consequences of her nihilism – to turn her away from completing her execution of Miles Dyson. First, she sees herself – a would-be assassin and killer of children, a destroyer of the human family, a terminator – in her victim's eyes; second, she learns from John's attempt to stop her that her failure to be a mother to her son has not annihilated his capacity to be a son to his mother, and hence not annihilated her capacity to acknowledge herself as his mother; and third, she learns from the terminator's acceptance of John's orders that even technology is not destiny. These three factors are not unconnected – hence their threefold impact occurs within a single scene in the film; for it is plain that, in her eyes, the ultimate cause of the death of the future is technology, which she understands as the expression of an essentially death-dealing masculinity. She sneers at Dyson for thinking that building SkyNet is a creative act, seeing it rather as the antithesis of genuine, life-giving creativity as represented by female generativity; but Dyson's willingness to sacrifice himself to destroy the technological origins of SkyNet, the terminator's willingness to sacrifice itself in the same cause, and her awareness of her failure properly to mother the product of her biological creativity, together suggest that technology is no more destined to deny life than biology is destined to affirm it. What matters is what human beings make of them, whether they acknowledge their creatureliness and its creations, or deny them. 'No fate but what we make.'

Since *Terminator 2* presents Sarah's knowledge of the future as the source of the deathliness in her and in her world, it must present her recovery of the future as a function of annihilating that knowledge. If she is to overcome herself, the future must become unknown. The film makes this release possible by determining that the indispensable basis of the research that leads to SkyNet, and thence to nuclear war, should be the remains of the first terminator, rescued by the CyberDine Corporation from the robotic metal press. It follows from this that the future's (and hence Sarah's) emancipation from doom can be achieved if all traces of the first terminator are destroyed. As befits a Cameron sequel, this destruction takes a doubled form: first, John tosses the pieces of the first terminator (stolen from CyberDine) into the furnace; then, the second instance of that first terminator invites Sarah to lower it into the same furnace – its self-sacrifice imitating that of its unknowing creator, the nearest it can achieve to self-termination (which its programming forbids). And Sarah herself takes hope from its example, allowing herself to think of its self-sacrifice as suggesting the falsity of its earlier view that 'it's in your nature to destroy yourselves': 'for if a machine can learn the value of human life, maybe we can too'.

Rather more interesting than this concluding moral, however, is what the concluding events of this film say about the relation between it and its predecessor. For, of course, in destroying any trace of the first terminator, and thereby erasing the narrative (of nuclear war followed by human resistance to extermination by machines) that it enabled, Terminator 2 destroys not only the future reality from which its own two terminators come; it destroys the possibility of any future 'Terminator' films, and it destroys the future which enabled the events of Terminator itself – the film which is its own source or origin, its indispensable past. In other words, Terminator 2 self-terminates, and in so doing, it self-terminates both Terminator and the 'Terminator' series.

This second sequel in Cameron's directorial career thus makes profoundly radical use of the power inherent in any sequel to rewrite the significance of the predecessor to which it is inevitably indebted, and to determine the possibilities it leaves open to any future sequel. But in this case, its exercise is not inherently vengeful or self-aggrandizing – as if driven by the anxiety of influence or inheritance; it is rather liberating or empowering. For just as it frees Sarah from her death-in-life, so it frees Cameron himself from the nihilistic narrative universe that he had created, and from the need to return to it in any further sequels. In short, it freed him from any sense of confinement by his own origins as a director, reopening his own cinematic future.

But in so doing, he certainly appears to have foreclosed one possible mode in which that future might be realized. For we saw earlier that the spatio-temporal disruptions made possible by the science fiction genre, and utilized with unusual power in Terminator's time travel narrative, functioned as a kind of internal representation of the disruption inherent in the experience of viewing science fiction movies as such (which might be defined as projections of a future world that is simultaneously a world past). Sarah's nihilism is Terminator 2's internal representation of that viewing condition – which suggests that, for Cameron, representations of the future as knowable, as picturable in a way indistinguishable from reality, are incitements to conflate our relationship to the past (over which we can exercise no control) with our relationship to the future, whose openness is a condition of our capacity to think of our own lives as significant. *Terminator 2*'s self-termination amounts to a refusal or transcendence of that incitement, and hence a denial of one of the determining characteristics of the genre it inhabits. It is, to say the very least, unsurprising that Cameron himself has thus far avoided any further work in that genre.

However, the displacements to which Cameron subjects the world of his first film in order to effect this self-transcendence also allow him to explore further another aspect of what one might call the ontology of film. This involves what *Terminator 2* has to say about Linda Hamilton's potential for stardom, about what has and can become of her on film. At the end of *Terminator*, just as her character was on the verge of self-transformation, so Hamilton herself appeared to have the chance of becoming a star; and by the end of *Terminator 2* she has demonstrated the depth of her capacity to make her character's physical, psychological and spiritual vicissitudes real on screen. The soft, unformed physique of the first film has become a sleek, streamlined weapon; the emotional vulnerability of her younger self has calcified, and is then recovered to reinform her renewed maternal impulses and her sense of hope for the unwritten future. And yet, despite this capacity to absorb and represent the complex and unsympathetic trajectory of her character, and to bear up under the physical demands of a typically pyrotechnic and kinetic Cameron blockbuster, we now know that Linda Hamilton did not become a star – that her specific physiognomy proved incapable of projecting a life in the movies free from the conjunction of character and director that first made the possibility of stardom real for her. Can we even begin to answer the question: why not?

Terminator 2 offers a certain understanding of what it is to be a film star that might at least help us to formulate this question more sharply. It follows from the film's doubling or splitting of the terminator role it inherits from its predecessor. On the one hand, we have the same actor representing a differently-programmed reiteration of his earlier 'character'; on the other, inhabiting the 'villain' role thereby left vacant, we have a new actor representing the next generation of terminators, whose distinctive capacity is to mimic anything it samples by physical contact. We might think of these two types of terminator as each embodying one of the two conflicting vectors of any mode of acting – the constancy of the individual actor beneath or behind his differing roles (a cause of much disorientation and humour in the film), and the bewildering variety of characters he is called upon to inhabit (as uncanny in its way as the T-1000's brief re-embodiment of every human being it impersonated in its death-throes at the foundry). If, however, following Cavell, we acknowledge that the relationship between these two vectors in screen acting is determined by the material basis of the medium, hence by the camera's automatic reproduction of the individual human physiognomy placed before it, then we would expect the actor to be prior to the character in film – with the individual actor lending himself to the character, accepting only that within it which fits, and discarding the rest (as opposed, say, to yielding himself to or working himself into the character, as might a theatre actor).[6] We should therefore expect stardom to turn more on an actor's constancy than his inconstancy, upon the effect of his physiognomic consistency across a body of films than upon any ability to change himself in accordance with the demands of an independently given part.

Against this background, it will seem rather less than accidental that, whilst Linda Hamilton's gift for inhabiting her character and its vicissitudes seems actually to have prevented her from attaining stardom, the actor whose appearance in both 'Terminator' films helped to project him into the highest reaches of cinematic fame was the one who, by playing the same, physically indistinguishable character, allowed the camera to transcribe and re-transcribe his utterly distinctive physiognomy without obstacle or interruption (and the one who, in his unparalleled ability to take physical direction, to do and hence to be exactly what his director wishes, earns from Cameron the label of 'the perfect actor'[7]) – Arnold Schwarzenegger.

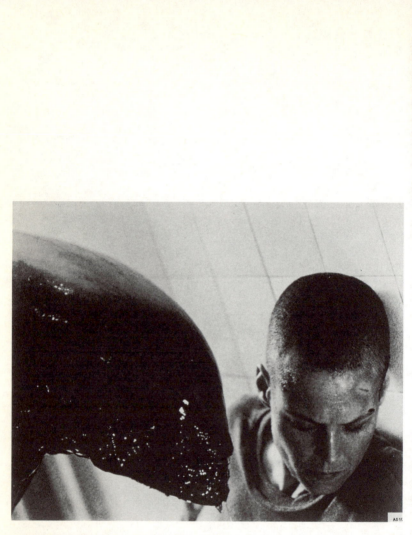

Alien³ © 1992 20th Century-Fox Film. Reproduced by courtesy of the Roland Grant Archive.

Mourning Sickness: David Fincher's *Alien³*

Three

If this film resembles its predecessor in any respect, it is in its rejection of the expected way of noting its own status within the series of 'Alien' films. James Cameron's title avoided the number '2' altogether (whilst discovering it obsessively within the film itself); David Fincher's incorporates the necessary numeral, but only after subjecting it to a radical displacement. In one respect, to present the number '3' as a superscript simply emphasizes the fact of the film's belatedness (its appearance after not one but two highly idiosyncratic directors have imposed their very different personal visions on a very distinctive original idea), as if Fincher feels that anything he might do with his film will be superscriptural, a writing over the writings of others, as if this third film in the series cannot but constitute a palimpsest. But such a constraint is also a liberation, a form of empowerment; for the creator of a palimpsest can either reiterate the work of his predecessors, or obliterate it without trace, or subject it to radical displacement. More specifically, the advantage of directing '*Alien* III' is that it means making a contribution to a series, not a sequel. For Cameron, there was no distinction between the 'Alien' universe and Ridley Scott's realization of it, or at least none until and through his own reworking of that original realization; but for Fincher, Cameron's response to his inheritance opens up the possibility of distinguishing in each case between the director and his material, and gives him the chance critically to evaluate the strengths and weaknesses of their specific inflections of that common subject matter. And given that Fincher's structural belatedness links him more closely to Cameron than to Scott (with his enviable, truly creative and ineliminable priority), we might expect him to be rather more sensitive to his immediate predecessor – rather more concerned to establish a critical distance between '*Alien* II' and '*Alien* III'.

But of course, to attach a number as a superscript to a preceding symbol typically denotes the result of a mathematical operation – that of multiplying the symbol by itself a given number of times. Applying this to *Alien*^{3}, we get: Alien x Alien x Alien. What might this indicate about the film thus named? To begin with, it acknowledges that the film is dealing with the third generation of the alien species (the alien stalking the convicts on Fiorina 161 is the offspring of the alien queen ejected from the *Sulaco*, who was herself the offspring of the alien queen who laid the eggs on LV 426), and it signals in advance that it will itself directly be concerned with three aliens (the facehugger on the *Sulaco*, the alien offspring of the convict's dog, and the new alien queen). It further suggests that the film takes itself to be a certain kind of intensification of the 'Alien' universe with which we are by now familiar: its nature has been determined only by those elements present in the first film in the series, all other (essentially extraneous) material has been eliminated, and what results is a kind of condensation or sublimation of the essence of the 'Alien' universe. Beyond this, we might recall that *Alien*^{3} could also be rendered 'Alien cubed' – and think of the coming film's unremitting emphasis upon various attempts to confine its alien (in a toxic waste container, in a maze of corridors, in a lead mould, and ultimately in a sheath of super-cooled lead).

The setting of these attempts – the oppressively enclosed, maximum security prison that is the film's world, and that is itself closed down in the film's epilogue – only intensifies the implication that Fincher's primary preoccupation as a director is with closure. His aim is not to open up the 'Alien' series but to shut it down; this step in its unfolding will be its last.

WE COMMIT THESE BODIES TO THE VOID

As if to underline this, Fincher opens $Alien^3$ with a title sequence that, in effect, ends the film. In a superbly-edited sequence of very brief, beautifully-composed shots intercut with the film's main titles, we see an alien facehugger (hatched from an egg left by the queen before her ejection) invade the *Sulaco*'s cryogenic compartment, penetrate Ripley's cryotube and attach itself to her face; some drops of the alien's acid blood start a fire in the compartment, and the ship automatically transfers all three cryotubes to one of the *Sulaco*'s emergency escape vehicles (EEV), which is then ejected and plummets into the atmosphere of Fiorina 161. As the vehicle crash-lands in water, we are told that the planet houses an Outer Veil mineral ore refinery which functions as a maximum-security work correctional facility for 'Double-Y chromosome' prisoners.

Each element in this opening sequence is very short, and sometimes difficult to grasp in all its implications, but the overall significance of the sequence is undeniable even on a first viewing: the fate against which Ripley has been struggling ever since her ordeal began, the worst possible incarnation of her nightmare vision of sexual difference and female generativity, has been realized before the film has even properly begun. From the moment we see her extracted from the EEV and placed on the operating table, identified as the only survivor of its crash-landing, we know that she is (as she later puts it, as if echoing Sarah Connor) 'already dead'; she cannot physically survive the alien's inevitable emergence, and since her deepest impulse throughout the series has been to stake her spiritual identity upon her refusal to be penetrated (whether by the alien or by men), neither can her psyche be expected to survive the knowledge of its introduction.

The sheer brutality of this opening is breathtaking in its audacity: Fincher has taken the full measure of our long-deepening identification with Ripley's capacity to handle herself, her powerful embodiment of the ideal of the nurturing warrior, and of the satisfaction we took in her apparent triumph at the end of *Aliens*, and utterly negated them. And everything that is to come in his narrative of Ripley's adventures on Fiorina 161 (as scripted by David Giler, Walter Hill and Larry Ferguson) has thereby been stripped of significance – her thoughts, deeds and experiences will amount at best to a kind of death-in-life. When measured against what has already happened to her, nothing of any true importance can happen to her except the gradually dawning realization of what has already happened to her – the realization that her life is already over.

Fincher thereby deprives himself of resources that one might hitherto have considered essential to the repertoire of any director working with this material – the capacity to maintain suspense or to generate narrative drive, the ability to manipulate the audience's desire to know what will happen next, to make the fate of one's protagonist appear to hang on the twists and turns of a plot. Fincher's relationship with his audience must, accordingly, differ radically from that of his predecessors – particularly James Cameron; by so forcefully refusing to satisfy the expectations we bring to his film, he forces on us (and upon himself) the question of what satisfactions we might hope for from a film from which hope has been so quickly and so decisively excised.

It is the general failure to recognize this opening sequence as Fincher's way of refusing familiar cinematic pleasures that accounts, in my view, for the relative lack of critical and commercial favour accorded this film in the series. Particular disappointment was expressed with the film's concluding half, in which Ripley and the convicts attempt in various ways to trap the alien in the maze-like corridors of the foundry: the audience acquires no overall sense of the geography of the refinery, and is barely capable of distinguishing one shaven-headed male from another before the alien catches and kills them, let alone of recognizing one strategically significant intersection of corridors or sealed door from its less fateful counterparts. But Fincher is not here trying, and failing, to generate the usual structure of suspense and fear: the terrain of this final hunting of the beast is unsurveyable, and the unfolding of its events is disorienting and uncompelling, because Fincher has always already lost (and has already done his utmost to deprive his audience of) any faith in the intrinsic significance of such narrative artifacts. The business of avoiding or trying to kill the beast comes across as meaningless because for Fincher it is meaningless; he has set up his 'Alien' universe in such a way that such sequences of events, in which reside the essence of storytelling (our telling of stories to one another, and our attempts to think of our own lives as narratives), appear only as irrelevant distractions. He is trying to tell us that the dimension of 'plot' – the inflections and outcome of interlinked events – is not where the heart of his, and our, interest in the 'Alien' universe should really lie.

The first phase of the film after its title sequence continues this brutal negation of our expectations by turning its attention to its immediate predecessor. As we have seen, James Cameron concluded *Aliens* by rewarding Ripley for her attainment of the ideal of the nurturing warrior by allowing her to acquire a family without having to acknowledge the fertility of her flesh. Fincher begins his film by not only depriving Ripley of both husband and child – she wakes to find them already dead, as if they had always been no more than a dream – but also forcing her to instigate an autopsy on Newt. The sequence in which Clemens is shown marshalling and deploying the surgical instruments needed to open up and display Newt's torso to Ripley's horrified gaze is almost unbearable in its intensity, as if Ripley herself is going under the surgeon's knife. But the true subject of this dispassionate dissection is in fact *Aliens*, and hence James Cameron; Fincher has, in effect, identified Cameron's pivotal contribution to the series and extirpated it from the 'Alien' universe as if it were not only dead but potentially infectious, as if *Aliens* (despite, or rather because of, its commanding invocation of the adrenaline-rush of action, suspense and narrative drive) had taken the series away from itself, condemning it (and any successor which accepted Cameron's terms for it) to inauthenticity and lifelessness. Fincher's autopsy finds no more trace of genuinely alien life in *Aliens* than Clemens finds in Newt; in performing that surgery, he is declaring that he intends to return the series to itself – to our seemingly unquenchable interest in its protagonist and her opponent, and to the metaphysical questions that have inspired and sustained their mutual fascination and repulsion.

Fincher's determination to cut to the metaphysical bone is declared in the culmination of this first portion or act of the film, which presents the cremation of Hicks and Newt in the foundry's furnaces. The scene is once again organized with great elegance and economy: Superintendent Andrews' more formal, merely dutiful pronouncement before the bodies are despatched is succeeded and overwhelmed by a heartfelt speech from Dillon, the leader of the convicts and the inspiration behind the 'apocalyptic, millenarian, Christian fundamentalism' that binds these criminals together in their self-imposed exile from the human world; and both are intercut with the alien's birth from its canine host (infected by a facehugger brought down in the EEV from the *Sulaco*).

Andrews speaks of the two bodies as having been 'taken from the shadow of our nights, released from all darkness and pain'; he articulates a mode of religious belief which conceives of itself as embodying a means of escaping or transcending suffering and death, a perspective from which their significance might be diminished or explained away. In contrast, Dillon asks

Why are the innocent punished? Why the sacrifice, why the pain? There aren't any promises, nothing is certain – only that some get called, some get saved. We commit these bodies to the void with a glad heart, for within each seed there is the promise of a flower; within each death, no matter how small, there is always a new life, a new beginning.

In effect, then, Dillon denies that his faith provides any answers to these questions, any solutions to these 'problems' – because human suffering is not a problem to be resolved or dissolved, as if even unmerited pain that is deemed essential to bringing about a greater good (as when Christian theology claims that the suffering of the innocent might be outweighed if it is part of a divine plan to achieve an overwhelming good for all humankind) were any less painful and undeserved for the innocent individual who is required to suffer it. Dillon knows that rain falls on the just and the unjust alike; the natural world is not so organized as to distribute rewards and punishment according to moral desert, and any adequate religious response to that world must acknowledge this.

For Dillon, then, human life is not comprehensible apart from its vulnerability to contingency, pain and death – the law of the body; hence authentic human existence is to be achieved not by denying or explaining away our embodied mortality, but by acknowledging its burdens. And these burdens include not just the world's independence of our will, but also that of the self (at the very least, the self that refuses this new vision of the world). Dillon talks of a new life, a new beginning – of a transformation of the human self; but he roots the promise of that new life in the death of the old self, and he talks of that old self as something from which we are saved, from which we are called.

The first claim implies that change and redemption can grow only from a full acknowledgement of the old – and his convict community makes manifest what he takes that to involve. For in staying together within the circumstances of their imprisonment, they acknowledge the justice of their punishment and hence acknowledge their own depravity, their identity as 'murderers and rapists of women'; but they also think of that specific depravity as internally related to human nature as such – as an aspect of an original human sinfulness beyond any individual exercise of the will towards evil. They thus attempt to live with, to inhabit, a radically bleak conception of themselves and their common human nature; it is only their struggle to 'tolerate the intolerable' that keeps them open to the possibility of transformation and rebirth. But his second, further claim is that this new life is not something we can call upon, invoke or initiate, from within ourselves –

it is something to which we are called; to be saved is to experience grace, a gratuitous exercise of God's transforming love that we neither merit nor control, but to which we can either close ourselves off or keep ourselves open.

Why, then, does Fincher edit the cremation scene so as to conjoin Dillon's words about a new life emerging from every death, no matter how small, with the new birth of alien life from the death of a dog? The flower that this promises is not likely to give anyone a glad heart. But the dog's owner answers his own question when he asks: 'What kind of animal would do this to a dog?' – any animal whose nature requires it. By reminding us that the alien will as happily impregnate non-human as human species, Fincher implies that life, the realm of the biological, with its unstoppable drive to survive and reproduce, and its equally ineliminable openness to death and extinction, is simply (no more and no less than) natural; the alien just does what its nature demands, and the threat of being preyed upon and of dying is not the intrusion of an utterly alien force into the life of a given species but rather its essence and precondition – part of what it means to be a part of the natural realm. Such matters are what flesh and blood is ineluctably heir to, and hence are not to be denied (as Andrews' Christianity attempts to deny them) but acknowledged (as Dillon's Christianity attempts to acknowledge them).

If, however, we must acknowledge our embeddedness in nature and in life, with all its arbitrary gifts and withdrawals (of lovers and children, of talent and fortune, of health and disease, of life and death), and its bequest to every living being of an apparently ineliminable drive for its own survival and satisfaction, the question remains: can any perspective on these matters simultaneously accept them as part of the human condition without collapsing into despair at the absurdity or meaninglessness of life? Can human beings fully acknowledge what and who they are and still affirm their lives as meaningful? Can Ripley?

By the end of the cremation scene, Ripley has been made to experience to the full the contingency of human life, its vulnerability to arbitrary shifts of fortune. Having lost the two people whose entirely fortuitous advent into her life held out any hope that her capacity to love and nurture others might be fulfilled, she now finds herself in a world that is itself bereft of any products of human culture more advanced than the Industrial Revolution – a world whose medieval living conditions force her to salvage scraps of malfunctioning technology from rubbish heaps, and even to shave her head and genitals. Fincher is reducing Ripley to bare skin and bone, in search of the ineliminable essence of who she is.

We already know, however, from the previous 'Alien' films, what that essence is, what singled her out from the *Nostromo*'s crew as the alien's worthy other and fuelled her duel with the queen: her nightmare vision of human sexuality and generativity. Hence Fincher's brutal stripping away of the inessential Ripley leaves us, and her, confronting a world that is the fullest possible realization of that nightmare: Fiorina 161 incarnates the world of her fears, the fantasies that make her who she is. It houses a community of men whose natures exactly embody the vision of masculinity that has driven her resolute protection of her sexual and physical integrity thus far. It incorporates an alien, whose stalking of the ducts and corridors of the prison merely incarnates the truth of the prison itself from her perspective, and with whom she has already lost her personal battle – not because of any lack of resolution on her part, but simply because of the alien's ability to exploit her vulnerability (specifically, her inability as a finite creature to maintain consciousness indefinitely). She has been drugged, raped and made pregnant; and her offspring's birth will be the death of her. Little wonder that she struggles to make her voice heard in this world, fighting against the torn lining of her throat and the convicts' horrified fixation on her femaleness rather than her individuality. Fincher is here once again coming to terms, or settling scores, with James Cameron; for *Aliens* also begins with Ripley enduring a hypersleep nightmare in which she has been impregnated by, and is about to give birth to, an alien. Cameron presents his film as giving Ripley the therapy she needs to wake from such nightmares; Fincher presents his film as awakening Ripley from Cameron's dream, his fantasy of what constitutes a fulfilled existence for his protagonist, and his fantasy of human life as something that with the right degree of effort on our part can be made to come out right. For Fincher, nothing – not even achieving the requisite degree of emotional resilience, the ideal combination of male warrior and female nurturer – can guarantee anyone a happy ending, or render them immune to accident or ill-fortune. And Ripley in particular is no more cut out for a happy domestic life than the convicts surrounding her are cut out for happy, fulfilling relations with women. What defines her is also what has condemned her to a life inhabited so deeply and for so long by the alien that she 'can't remember anything else'. In this sense, Ripley is not just one of the alien family (as she expresses it, and as Fincher implies when his camera stresses the family resemblance of their physiognomies), she is the alien; it incarnates the nightmare that makes her who she is, and that she has always been incubating. Hence the alien in *Alien*[3] appears more as a loitering carnivore, killing time by killing prey, than as a parasite: its own capacity to reproduce is utterly dependent on the successful outcome of Ripley's pregnancy – as if Ripley herself is its queen, the source of its own life. Hence, too the film presents Ripley's own nature or identity as at once a maze through which she is condemned to run without hope of escape and as yearning to break out from its confinement within her – as something she encloses that is closing inexorably around her.

What, then, are we to make of the fact that in *Alien*[3] Ripley not only experiences heterosexual intercourse for the first time, but initiates it, and appears to regard it as enjoyable and fulfilling? Is this not entirely out of character for someone with her perspective on the nature of human sexuality – particularly so soon after the funeral of her closest companions? Everything turns here on the immediate and general contexts of the relevant scene. Most obviously, it occurs immediately after Fincher has deprived Ripley of her nonbiological family and forced her to confront the surgically displayed physical reality of female flesh and blood (in the form of Newt's autopsied body). Against this background, Ripley's sex with Clemens appears as an attempt to seek emotional comfort in sexual contact with a man – as if Fincher's brutal inversions of Cameron's alien universe (his rejection of Cameron's identification with, and indulgence of, Ripley's horrified aversion to the biological reality of sexual intercourse and maternity) have brought her to overcome her previous abhorrence of human embodiedness as such.

However, this triumph of Fincher's shock therapy is very short-lived: after all, Clemens is almost immediately slaughtered by the alien, who then takes over the role of Ripley's protector – quite as if its phallic violence and exclusive interest in its own offspring were a more accurate representation of the nature of sexual partnership than Clemens' gentle goodwill. Fincher's broader framing of the scene appears to confirm this; for it is preceded by Ripley's rape and impregnation by the alien, succeeded by her giving birth to its offspring, and is itself displaced by an act of murderous aggression (we see Ripley ask Clemens if he is attracted to her, and we see him thank her afterwards, but the space between is occupied not by a romantic representation of their lovemaking but by the alien's first and lethal attack on a prisoner). He thus equates the sex between Ripley and Clemens with Ripley's impregnation by an alien – as if confirming the inescapability of Ripley's own perception of heterosexual intercourse as a murderous assault, of pregnancy as a parasitic infestation, and of birth as the body's lethal betrayal of itself. The fact that the alien appears immediately after Clemens' second penetration of her body (with a hypodermic syringe) only reinforces this; it is as if, by allowing the sexual penetration of her body, Ripley has violated the virginity on which she conceives that her power to repel the alien rests, and hence has invited the alien back into her world. She cannot escape from herself that easily.

The full significance of the film's equation of the Ripley–Clemens encounter with the earlier Ripley–alien encounter emerges only if we ask whether Ripley really is utterly unaware of what happened to her in hypersleep. After all, there is evidence even in the title sequence that the facehugger's penetration disturbs her sleep, as if leaving some trace of itself in her subconscious mind; and the process by which she comes to realize what happened can as easily be seen as one of overcoming her initial repression of that fact as of discovering something entirely new to her. We can accept that her morning sickness might appear as the symptoms of excessive hypersleep; but how could she fail to understand the significance of the alien's refusal to attack her after killing

Clemens, or to draw from Bishop's confirmation of an active alien presence on board the *Sulaco* the conclusion that – since Newt and Hicks were free of infection – she must have been the victim? Certainly, her reaction to the conclusive, horrifying neuroscanner image is barely tinged with surprise.

Suppose, then, that from her first moments on Fiorina 161, Ripley is – at some level – aware that she has already been the subject of sexual penetration; then two further ways of understanding her sudden, unprecedented desire to have sex emerge.

According to the first, her sexual intercourse with Clemens is a symptomatic repetition of that original encounter – just what one would expect of someone presently unable fully to acknowledge a deeply traumatic experience. This sudden compulsion is her body's way of at once declaring and concealing what has happened to it, and to her: she is driven to enact the one deed whose nature makes it both an exact representation of the original trauma and a perfect cover-story for it.

According to the second reading, by contrast, Ripley's original impregnation by the alien is what makes it possible for her to have humanly meaningful sex with Clemens. After all, the nurturing warrior of *Aliens* (and even the cat-lover of *Alien*) is hardly bereft of the ordinary human desire to give and receive love; she is simply horrified by the physicality of its natural medium or means of expression, in which it can be literally as well as metaphorically creative, and hence is incapable of consciously acting so as to achieve what she desires. But in the world of *Alien*[3], as defined by its title sequence, Ripley has, without willing it, already undergone her worst nightmare of heterosexual intercourse and survived; hence (assuming she knows this about herself), it is a world in which actual, human heterosexual intercourse has been demystified, and hence become a real option for her.

The calm self-confidence with which Sigourney Weaver plays the scene with Clemens (the warm matter-of-factness with which she voices her invitation) suggests that the second of these readings is the correct one – that her sex with Clemens is a brief but intense achievement of self-overcoming (confirming that the truth about human sexuality is concealed by the incarnate nightmare of alien impregnation), rather than a symptomatic validation of her present self-understanding (confirming that alien impregnation incarnates the monstrous truth about human sexuality). In the end, however, that achievement is quickly rendered otiose; the reality she must confront is one in which Clemens is dead and she is host to an alien queen – in which the briefly glimpsed truth about human sexuality has been obliterated by the making real of her nightmare. What matters now is how she responds to that massive reiteration.

At first, her reaction is suicidal; but since, as she puts it, 'I can't do what I should', she tries to enlist the help of others – first by inviting the alien's lethal attentions, then by trying to get Dillon to re-enact one side of the mutual extermination pact she originally made with Hicks. He refuses – entirely unsurprisingly, since Christianity regards suicide as the worst of all sins, the sin against the Holy Spirit: it is the ultimate expression of despair, in which the sinner turns in upon herself in such a way as definitively to exclude God. In Dillon's terms, the suicide does not so much acknowledge her sinful self as allow it entirely to enclose and overwhelm her, and thereby closes herself off from the possibility of grace. By at first pretending to accede to her request, and then striking his fire-axe against the cell bars on which she is outstretched, he intends to teach her to overcome this impulse, to see that she can survive its grip on her, and turn her circumstances to good account.

And this, indeed, is what she does; her invulnerability to the alien's attentions is indispensable to the final success of the convicts' attempts to destroy it. But then she faces her final ordeal: the arrival of the Company's scientific team. She has prevented them capturing the warrior alien; but the queen is moving inside her. Bishop II, who claims to be the human designer of the android series, offers to arrange for its surgical extraction and destruction, holding out to her the chance of having a life, having children, and knowing that the alien is dead. But Ripley does not – she cannot – trust him: instead, she falls backwards, arms outstretched, into the furnace that recently swallowed the bodies of her husband and child. As she descends into the flames, the alien queen bursts out; Ripley holds it gently in her gloved hands, and lays its crowned head on her breast, as if to suckle it.

The logic of the 'Alien' universe, and of Ripley's own nature, is here finally consummated. Since the alien itself originates from within her, since it is an incarnate projection of her deepest fears, she can succeed in eliminating it only by eliminating herself. And their joint elimination amounts to the elimination of the 'Alien' universe itself, since their joint presence has made it what it is; it is as if, after its expansive, affirmative phase in *Aliens*, this monstrous cosmos has been subjected to a contraction so radical that only its absolute annihilation can constitute an adequate conclusion. The achievement of closure here, so absolute and on so many levels at once, has an elegance that almost disguises its nihilism.

But are we, in the end, meant to see Ripley's achievement as her elimination of herself, or as her elimination of that in herself which dictated the nature of the alien and its universe? Has she simply destroyed herself, or is her self-destruction also a self-overcoming? After all, literally speaking, her death destroys the source of alien life within her, and indeed is the only way in which it might be destroyed; and she plainly gives comfort and succour to the alien queen in its first and last moments of life outside the womb – quite as if she has undergone the realization of her worst nightmare of birth, and not only survived it but found herself capable of mothering her offspring. To be sure, she soothes it in silence, as if rendered mute by her fate; but her fall is succeeded by the film's concluding reproduction of her concluding mayday message from the *Narcissus*, as if her last deed might amount to the recovery of that first accession to her own voice, in despite of her alien other. And the Christian imagery of her death – Fincher's presentation of her death-dive as a crucifixion through which the human race is redeemed – further asks whether we can find anything life-affirming in this self-immolation.

Dillon certainly would. For in the eyes of his community, the alien was a dragon, a demonically powerful murderer and rapist whose very nature placed them in the position inhabited by the victims of their own crimes – in short, it was an incarnate projection of their sinfulness. Hence Ripley's refusal simply to allow the alien to reproduce itself through her, to act as a vehicle for its onward transmission through the human world, exemplifies the community's motive for remaining on Fiorina 161 – their collective resolve to acknowledge the sinfulness within them, to prevent themselves from reproducing it, and to await the grace that might allow them to overcome it. For Dillon, Ripley's actions would declare that she has received that grace – that she has been saved from herself, called to imitate Christ; she has taken the sinfulness of the community upon herself even unto death, and the purity of her self-sacrifice holds out the promise of redemption.

But can we really see the absolute closure of the 'Alien' universe as a new beginning? What might it mean, in such a world, to believe in the resurrection of the body?

WE ARE NOT WHAT WAS INTENDED

David Fincher's next (his second) film, with its focus on the hunt for a serial killer each of whose victims dies in a manner intended to exemplify one of the seven deadly sins, plainly develops further the interests which first found expression in *Alien*[3] – in questions about the significance of religious belief, the possibility of making human sense of human life and of the world human beings make and inhabit, the idea of closure and its overcoming. But *Se7en* undeniably shows that Fincher is perfectly capable of utilizing narrative conventions when he wants to: it has a tightly-organized and utterly gripping plot (written by Andrew Kevin Walker), in which its two detective protagonists race against time to locate and interpret the clues which will indicate not only the identity of the killer but the nature of his intentions before he can carry them out. But it also excels at manipulating the generic expectation of its audience (most famously with its climax, in which both the detectives and the killer are woven into the sequence of events they would normally be attempting either to prevent or to complete from the outside, as it were); and it is, at the most fundamental level, a critical study of the conditions which makes such generic exercises possible – in particular, a study of the assumption that the killer's intentions and actions might make any sense, and hence of what it is for human actions as such to have any meaning whatever.

It is fundamental to the approach that Detective Somerset (Morgan Freeman) takes to this case that the killings they encounter are not just deeds – merely more instances of the utterly unthinking, mindlessly brutal things human beings do to one another. They have a meaning, and if Somerset can understand their meaning, understand what the killer is trying to say in and through his treatment of his victims, then he might be able to predict their course and identify their perpetrator. What, then, is John Doe trying to say? What is the meaning of his tableaux?

It is tempting to answer that, in each case, an individual who is guilty of a particular deadly sin is murdered in a manner that confirms his guilt, and that simultaneously functions as a religious admonition to the broader human community in which such sinful behaviour is pervasive, and accepted without criticism or question – even lauded. However, one difficulty with this interpretation is that the dead are not in each case guilty of the relevant sin (in the 'Lust' murder, it is surely not the prostitute but her client who is lustful); another is that those who are guilty do not always die (this is true not only of the lustful client, but also of Victor Allen, the 'Sloth' victim, and of Detective Mills, the exemplar of 'Wrath'). We might further question whether John Doe can simply be described as murdering any of his victims. What he rather does is offer them a choice: either he will kill them or they must perform an action exemplary of the sin he imputes to them (keep eating, cut off a pound of their own flesh, keep taking the drugs, have sex wearing a serrated dildo). In each case, their choice relieves him of the need to murder them: they rather kill themselves, choosing to act in the way that John Doe believes has already destroyed them spiritually, even when that action will result in their psychological and/or physical destruction. It might be more accurate to call this assisted suicide, or at least assisted self-destruction.

This description certainly fits the first four crimes (gluttony, greed, sloth, lust); it doesn't exactly fit the 'Pride' case, but here John Doe gives his victim the opportunity to phone for help, and she chooses to die of her injuries instead, so he is even less obviously her murderer; and in the 'Envy' and 'Wrath' cases, John Doe chooses his own death rather than refrain from an act expressive of his sinful envy (the beheading of Mills' wife), and Mills chooses his own psychological and moral self-destruction rather than refrain from wreaking vengeance on Doe.

We cannot, therefore, take Doe's sermons simply to enact Old Testament wrath – as if their religious meaning is that of executing divine sentences of death (after all, wrath is not the sin with which he identifies himself). The moral of his address to the community seems rather to be: our sinfulness is pervasive, and deeply rooted in (original to) our natures, and it is killing us; even when it is not literally lethal, it kills the soul, the human spirit within us. My sermons are meant to make that self-destructiveness unmissably concrete, and thereby to give us a last chance of understanding what we are doing to ourselves, what we have become, and thus give us a last chance to do otherwise. As he puts it in the excerpt Somerset reads from his notebooks, 'we are nothing; we are not what was intended'.

Note the 'we': Doe is not exempting himself from his diagnosis, as he could not in all consistency, given his sense of the absolute pervasiveness of sin. His sermons thus incorporate himself; their completion or closure depends upon his own willingness to be punished for his envy of Mills' normal life, and his inclusion further implies that the whole cycle or sequence is an expression of envy. In what sense? In part, it is an envy of God – since Doe arrogates to himself the privilege of judging and punishing the souls of others that Christianity reserves to God alone; but more generally, it indicates Doe's belief that although he does what he does out of love, that love (which finds expression in the systematic torture and murder of other human beings, the willingness to make them suffer for what he deems to be a greater good) is essentially misdirected (as misdirected as Andrews' conception of the Christian God in *Alien*[3]). This is made clear by one of the texts that Somerset is seen photocopying in the library: it displays an intellectual topography of Dante's purgatory, in which all seven of the deadly sins are seen as distorted expressions of love – gluttony, lust and greed as forms of excessive love, sloth as a (in fact, the only) form of deficient love, and pride, envy and wrath as forms of misdirected love. (Hence, in every deadly sin, each expression of our failure to be what was intended, we can see what Doe thinks we were originally intended to be – beings constituted by properly proportioned and rightly directed love.)

If John Doe does not exempt himself from his own diagnosis, neither does he exempt the detectives pursuing him, and hence the forces of law and order as such. Mills is directly incorporated into the sermons, because Doe recognizes that his otherwise admirable zeal to do the right thing, to catch and punish those who do wrong, is not properly proportioned or targeted – it can all too easily be turned upon his colleagues, his wife, even a humble newspaper photographer. And although the film in many ways opposes the character of Mills to that of Somerset, Mills' maintenance of that zeal to do good is the one aspect of his character as a detective of which

Somerset is himself envious (and hence, in this respect, indistinguishable from Doe); in him, that zeal is not so much better proportioned or directed as on the point of extinction. Somerset's personal oasis of calm and order in the city's chaos is an attempt to exclude the world, and hence an expression of his sense of his own exclusion from that world, his freedom from its spiritual disorder; but when Mills makes his most unguarded declaration of his commitment to law and order in a bar, and accuses his partner of giving up on that commitment, Somerset implicitly acknowledges this critique by hurling away his metronome.

But of course, the complicity of the forces of law and order in the sinful world that Doe diagnoses is more pervasive than this. For most of Mills' and Somerset's colleagues appear to share the moral apathy of the city's population as a whole: every crime is just another job, of no human significance, eliciting no vestige of empathy with its victims and bystanders and no particular condemnation of its perpetrator; this endless cycle of violence done and suffered is just what life is like, just the way it always has been and always will be. They are therefore constitutionally incapable of understanding Doe's enterprise as anything other than an extension of this cycle: more meaningless killing, more human lunacy. Hence, he provides them with a perfect candidate for the role of criminal – Victor Allen, whose upbringing and record exactly fit the psychological profile of a serial killer, right down to the fingerprinted plea for help found at the scene of the 'Greed' crime. Allen instead turns out to be the next victim – someone whose brain has been destroyed, and who exemplifies not only his own addiction to 'Sloth' but that of the police who are led unthinkingly to him. From Doe's viewpoint, an even better word for this sloth and apathy would be 'despair', the ultimate sin.

The question then arises: how far is the film itself complicit with Doe's perception of the world? How far can Fincher be said to have orchestrated his film so as to endorse the killer's viewpoint? Certainly, the film seems no less harshly to condemn the apathy that pervades its city than does Doe, since the highly sympathetic character of Somerset embodies that condemnation, and proposes as its only alternative exactly what Doe proposes – a properly directed love, a love which 'costs, it takes effort, work'. But even the film's most moving and beautifully-realized vision of a life in which love is at work – the marriage of David and Tracy Mills – is shown to be threatened by its opposite, both from without (invaded by noise, unwilling to risk investing in its own future by bringing a child into the world) and within (Tracy's secrets, David's wrathfulness).

On the other hand, the film is also deeply marked by the oppositions that it sets up between Mills and Somerset, and some of these oppositions help to distance it from Doe's self-understanding. The list of these oppositions is long (country v. city; youth v. age; black v. white; noise v. silence; children v. childlessness), but much of it involves variations on a single distinction – that between deeds and their meaning. Mills wants only to know what was done; he thinks that simply looking at the dead body should allow him to read the identity of the killer directly off it; he has no interest in small details but in the basic, self-evident general shape of a situation. Somerset responds primarily to what a deed or situation might mean; he assumes that its true meaning will be hidden, difficult to interpret, and that significance can be squeezed indefinitely out of every small detail of a situation. Hence, Mills is entirely bemused by, and excluded from, those aspects of the human form of life in which meaning is focused, preserved and refined – libraries and the books they contain, religion, literature, music – what one might call human culture as such. Somerset is a citizen of this realm, an adept of scholarship; and the structures of significance that he lives and breathes are what make it possible for him and his partner to follow the clues that lead to John Doe.

But of course, the clue that leads them both to John Doe's door is an FBI printout of the killer's library borrowings. In other words, John Doe is as much an adept of culture, of human practices of meaning-making and meaning-trans-mission, as is Somerset; they not only live in the same world, they have read the same books; the resources that Somerset deploys to locate Doe are the very resources he deploys in constructing his criminal tableaux. Dantean topography and Thomist theology allow us to understand what Doe's crimes mean because they were capable of constituting a blueprint for it; Doe's murderous activity can be mistaken for the work of a performance artist because human culture as such embodies the results of the labours of the best thinkers and artists of the race to build significance into and out of the most savage, brutal and base aspects of human existence, to make the meaningless meaningful.

Suppose, then, as Mills would have us do, that instead of approaching Doe's tableaux as cultural constructs, directing our energies to the uncovering or decoding of the significance he labours to build into his deeds, we instead strip out his aesthetically and intellectually pleasing symmetries and symbolisms and look at what he has actually done. (Within the film, Mills does this by looking at photographs of the crime scene, transcriptions that confront us with the thing itself and not some surrogate or symbol of it – as if cinema is inherently, materially drawn to seeing the world as Mills sees it.) What we then see is the butchering of human flesh and blood. What Doe means to say is inscribed upon the bodies of his victims; hence, what he says and what he shows differ radically. He talks of spiritual suicide; but his sermons show the reducibility of human life to flesh (gluttony), blood (greed), skin and bone (sloth), sexuality (lust), a skull and its contents (pride, envy, wrath). The severed head of Doe's final sermon does not merely represent or encapsulate envy and wrath; it is the material basis of the human capacity to represent the world at all, to see it as meaningful, and its detachment from the body literalizes the detachment from material reality that such constructions of culture can seem to embody.

Doe's work is indeed full of meaning, as all human works are; but it is also strictly, intrinsically senseless – not merely the work of an unhinged mind, a lunatic, but an apotheosis of the distinctively human capacity to make meaning, a capacity whose exercise disguises from us the essential meaninglessness of the reality that is both its object and its source. This is why Doe is shown to have filled 200 250-page notebooks; a team of officers working seven-day weeks around the clock would take years simply to get to the end of them. The problem is not that meaning is hard to find in Doe's deeds, but that it is far too easy – his acts are full to overflowing with meaning, unsurveyably saturated in it; their most basic significance lies in their incarnation of the self-asphyxiating excess of signification that makes the human species what it is.

This sense of our humanity as being under threat from the very capacity that civilizes or humanizes us, of being hermetically sealed within our own systems of signification, is what gives such an apocalyptic atmosphere to the film's climax. For in Doe's final tableau, the meaning of his deeds suddenly, shockingly expands to ingest not only him but his two pursuers;[1] his sermons thereby not only swallow up good as well as evil, but also fuse the usually distinct generic functions of victim, perpetrator and pursuer – the orthodox narrative structure and drive of which this film seems to be a beautiful exemplar turns out to provide the condition for its own annihilation. On every level, no matter how closely we look, closure reigns.

Little wonder, then, that Fincher ends his title sequence with a subliminal glimpse of the following scratched phrase – 'No Key'. It tells us before we start that there will be no way out of this narrative, that there is no particular insight or super-clue that will make final sense of Doe's deeds (in part because they have no meaning, in part because they mean too much), that there can be no key to the meaning of anything in human life – and indeed to the meaning of human life as such – because it is essentially meaningless (the natural product of natural causes, just one piece of the unstoppable, blind machinery that is nature, that system in which things and creatures just do what they do).

In this sense, a religious perspective is no more significant than any other perspective – its implications no more worthy of serious contemplation. And yet. . . . If it is the seamless closure of the film's final scene that conveys this message to us, then we should note that, in fact, Doe's final sermon does not and cannot guarantee its own completion; indeed, we might rather argue that its most important moral is meant to be that the closure it represents is humanly avoidable, and that this is Christianity's deepest significance. For of course, Doe's sermons achieve closure only because Mills acts wrathfully; confronted with the knowledge of what Doe has done to his wife and unborn child, and hence done to him, he chooses to take revenge – to hurt the one who hurt him. But he could have chosen otherwise: he could have resolved to step back from that entirely natural human response, to allow the endless cycle or transmission mechanism of pain inflicted on one person being in turn inflicted on another, and so on another, to find its end in him. He could, in short, have suffered without himself inflicting suffering (as Ripley ends her life by doing). He did not; but, as Somerset realizes, Doe's sermon could not have attained closure if Mills had refrained from doing unto others as they had done unto him (and the other elements of Doe's sermon would have been equally definitively sabotaged if his victims had chosen not to do what came naturally to them, not to continue sinning).

What Doe, and hence *Se7en*, thereby delineates by negation is the distinctively Christian moral ideal we first encountered in *Alien*[3] – that of turning the other cheek, of breaking the seemingly endless sequence of human wrongdoing. But should we dwell on what is thereby delineated, or upon the fact that it is delineated by negation? If, in Fincher's cinematic world, Christianity and nihilism are each other's negation, and hence neither is representable without simultaneously representing the other, should we conclude that nihilism is the only way of achieving a truly thoroughgoing denial of Christianity, or that Christianity has always already acknowledged the worst that nihilism can tell us?

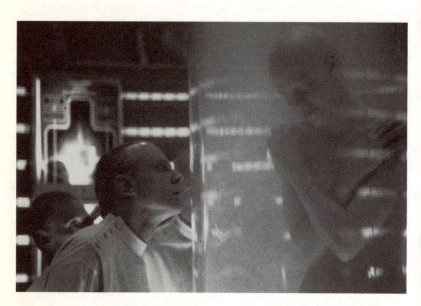

Alien Resurrection © 1997 20th Century-Fox Film. Reproduced by courtesy of the Roland Grant Archive.

The Monster's Mother: Jean-Pierre Jeunet's
Alien Resurrection

Four

Is *Alien Resurrection* a sequel to *Alien*[3], and hence to the previous two 'Alien' films? It may seem that the presence of the aliens, together with that of Sigourney Weaver as Ripley, guarantees this; but in fact, it merely displaces the question. For can we simply take it for granted that the aliens are the same species that we encountered in the earlier films, or that the Ripley of *Alien Resurrection* is the same person whose vicissitudes we have followed from their beginning on the *Nostromo*? After all, David Fincher's furious, purifying desire for closure in *Alien*[3] resulted in the death of Ripley and of the sole surviving representative of the alien species inside her. Hence Jeunet's film, helping itself to the resources for self-renewal that science fiction makes available to its practitioners, can recover the queen and her host only by positing the capacity to clone them from genetic material recovered from the medical facilities on Fiorina 161. But as his renegade military scientists make clear at the outset, the cloning process produces another, distinct individual from this genetic material; it does not reproduce the individual from whom the material derives. Their clone of the original Ripley is not Ripley herself – her body is not Ripley's body (however much it resembles the one consumed in Fiorina's furnace), and her mind has no inherent continuity with Ripley's (it must be stocked from her own experiences). As Call puts it, she is 'a strain, a construct; they grew you in a fucking lab'.

To be sure, as the film progresses the clone begins to recover some access to Ripley's memories and character; but that results from an aspect of her nature that reinforces her distinctness from her genetic original. For of course, one cannot even regard Ripley's clone as human – as a member of the same species as Ripley herself. She has acid for blood, her flesh is capable of accelerated healing, her sense of smell is highly developed, and she possesses an intuitive awareness of the thoughts and deeds of the aliens surrounding her. She is, in fact, neither fully human nor fully alien, but rather a hybrid – a creature whose genetic base is constituted by a grafting of human and alien stock (consequent upon the foetal alien queen's parasitic interactions with Ripley's flesh and blood); and one manifestation of that hybridity – her participation in the alien species' hive mind and racial memory – makes it possible for her to recall Ripley's life and death.

If Ripley's clone is not Ripley, can we say that the cloned alien queen within her is identical with her genetic original, the last surviving alien entity? Questions of personal identity may seem less pressing, as well as less clear, with respect to a species for whom the collective is prior to (and indeed eclipses) the individual; but what of species identity? If the queen is the new fount and origin of alien life in Jeunet's universe, within which two hundred years have passed since the original alien species was rendered extinct, should we regard her fertility as engendering the simple reproduction of that earlier race? In fact, we cannot – because the cloned queen is not exactly the pure origin of this new manifestation of alien life, and hence her reproductive cycle turns out to be anything but a simple replication of its monstrous original. For the queen's genetic hybridity incorporates a distinctively human gift from Ripley to her offspring (the gift bequeathed by original sin to all human females) – that of pregnancy, labour and birth. 'In sorrow shalt thou bring forth children.'

Jeunet's film thus finds a way of grafting two apparently opposed or contradictory modes of reproduction onto one another. Cloning suggests replication, qualitative indistinguishability, whereas hybridity suggests the cultivation of difference, a new creation. In *Alien Resurrection*, cloning engenders hybridity; even genetic replication cannot suppress nature's capacity for self-transformation and self-overcoming, its evolutionary impulse. This film does not, then, overcome *Alien*^{3}'s attempted closure of the 'Alien' series by resurrecting either Ripley or her alien other – as if continuing (by contesting) David Fincher's theological understanding of the alien universe; for (as Thomas' sceptical probing of Jesus' resurrected body implies) the religious idea of resurrection incorporates precisely the bodily continuity that cloning cannot provide. The title of Jeunet's film thus refers not to a resurrection of the alien species, or of that species' most intimate enemy; it rather characterizes its hybrid of cloning and hybridity as an alien kind or species of resurrection – as something uncannily other to any familiar religious idea of death's overcoming.

And of course, Jeunet thereby characterizes his film's relation to its predecessors as itself alien or unfamiliar: since neither of its cloned protagonists are identical with the paired protagonists of the earlier 'Alien' films, *Alien Resurrection* cannot be understood simply as a sequel to them. Its alien universe is at once utterly discontinuous with, and intimately dependent upon, them; its underlying thematic and stylistic codes owe everything and nothing to their templates. In grafting his own distinctive cinematic sensibility onto that of the series he inherits, Jeunet thereby sees himself as creating a world whose nature is built from the same components, but in a radically new manner – a hybrid clone of its ancestor; and hence he sees himself as following out a hybrid cloning of the idea of sequel-hood that has been established by the series hitherto. For to take *Alien*[3] seriously is to acknowledge that no further development of the series is possible in the terms shared by its three members; its further evolution requires their displacement. Only in such a way – only by transposing the central themes of the 'Alien' series into a new key – could Jeunet acknowledge the depth and completeness of Fincher's closure of the series without accepting its finality.

SEEING WITH THE EYES OF A CHILD

In establishing the transfigured terms of his alien universe, Jeunet naturally draws upon the cinematic sensibility manifest in his two previous films (in partnership with Marc Caro – hence, already itself a hybrid sensibility): *Delicatessen* and *The City of Lost Children*. Indeed, the family resemblances between the world of the latter film and that of *Alien Resurrection* go far beyond the fact that the central roles of both are taken by the same actors. Its narrative concerns the efforts of a quasi-scientific team, most of whom are clones of one of the team's co-founders, to expropriate the dream-life of orphan children, who are otherwise exploited by a variety of freakish human adults for more straightforwardly criminal purposes. These opposing but equally abusive stratagems are confounded by a small band of children, led by a strong-willed brown-haired girl, who join forces with a circus strongman named One – a simple-minded but morally pure giant, a child in an adult's body, whose basic motivation is to save his young brother from the scientists. In the world of this city, human flesh is variously deformed or mutilated, essentially unstable and subject to transformation – as if accentuating the uncanniness of the animated human body, with its internal relation to animality and its ability to incorporate the inanimate. One set of criminal forces is led by two women whose torsos are fused together, and includes a man who regards a set of killer fleas as if they were his children; another utilizes a religious sect whose members graft prosthetic devices onto their bodies to enhance vision and hearing; and the scientific team includes a brain in a vat. Technology pervades the culture, but in forms which execute their intended (and usually sinister) tasks by means of absurdly over-elaborate arrangements of highly primitive parts – as if implicitly mocking their adult creators' hubristic self-satisfaction in their own intelligence and creativity.

The correspondences between this universe and that of *Alien Resurrection* are overwhelming. The band of pirates from the *Betty*, whose purposes initially include the sale of living human bodies to a scientific team whose cloning programme requires them as hosts, but ultimately converge with the moral vision of the petite brunette robot Call, constantly manifest a child-like delight in weaponry and the unselfconscious satisfaction of physical appetite (exemplified in *The City of Lost Children* by One's brother and his insatiable desire for food). They include a disabled engineer, parts of whose wheelchair reassemble into a weapon, a not-so-gentle giant, and a weapons expert whose hidden pistols are mounted on extensible metal limbs; and Ripley's clone strides at their head with the physical and moral purity, the genetic and spiritual charisma, of One amongst his new brothers and sisters. Furthermore, the highly advanced technologies of the *Auriga* – the security system based on breath identification, the whisky-defrosting device, and the pointlessly extended well through which the guards observe Ripley's clone – are tainted with absurdity and primitivism.

The world of *Alien Resurrection* is, then, undeniably an

inflection of Jeunet's world; but can it properly be regarded as even a hybrid clone of the alien universe established by the earlier films? That universe has certainly hitherto conceived of science as threatening, and of technology as a necessary but feared supplement to vulnerable human flesh and blood; but it has not imagined either as absurd or risible, or elicited a kind of dark hilarity from the body's fragility (as Jeunet finds when Johnner allows his knife to bury itself in Vriess' paralysed leg, or when an alien warrior punches through General Perez' skull, or when Dr Wren's torso is penetrated by an alien bursting from the chest of the last surviving human host), or exhibited such unquestioning assurance in the robustness of humanity (and of our capacity to acknowledge it) under even the most extreme mutations of its embodiment. In these respects, Jeunet's cinematic sensibility can seem profoundly dissonant with that of the previous 'Alien' films – as if his contribution to the series is a kind of parody or caricature, in which matters that his predecessors have treated as being of profound and horrifying moment appear as ridiculous or trivial.

This impression has contributed greatly to the relatively low esteem in which *Alien Resurrection* is held by many who think highly of the other members of the series.[1] But there is good reason to contest its accuracy – or at least, its present critical monopoly; and we can begin to see why if we recall further relevant facets of Jeunet's previous work. To begin with, *The City of Lost Children* presents a world of absent or perverse parental figures (the children of the city are either orphaned or adopted by the malevolent Octopus, the woman whom the clones call 'Mother' is only their original's wife, and One's father dies in the film's opening scenes), in which adult sexuality appears as disgusting and dangerous (One's sole encounter with a sexually attractive woman is seen as a threat to his moral purity, the occasion only for a temptation to betray his true companions and friends, the band of children and particularly his adopted sister Miette). In these respects, Jeunet's world and that of the 'Alien' series are deeply attuned; as we have seen, the Ripley who dies on Fiorina 161 is one for whom motherhood is variously absent, displaced or repressed – its preconditions and condition (that is, human heterosexuality and generativity, the fecundity of the flesh) understood as a threat to her physical and spiritual integrity, as her monstrous other.

Moreover, the form and style of Jeunet's earlier film suggests a certain kind of generic justification for his preoccupation with these thematic matters, and offers a way of understanding his otherwise bewildering mode of appropriation of the alien universe. For *The City of Lost Children* is plainly a fantasy or fairy tale; it tells a story in which children are the central protagonists, and it presents the world they inhabit from their viewpoint. This is why the adults in this world appear as essentially grotesque – their purposes either obscure, ridiculous or opposed to the interests of children, their technological and religious preoccupations patently absurd, their relation to their own most natural appetites hedged round with prohibition and distortion, their sexual natures utterly incomprehensible. Hence, the children in this film treat the absence of their parents with equanimity, and invest themselves in the maintenance of relationships with other children, and most importantly with siblings – children who are also family (whether real or imagined), and hence the apotheosis of asexual intimacy. Accordingly, One searches unceasingly for his lost little brother, and adopts Miette as his little sister; and Miette shows her worthiness by being prepared to sacrifice herself to rescue One's brother from the demonic dream-landscape of her world's worst adult, a sacrifice she thinks of as her way of acquiring a brother (One's brother, and One himself).

We might think of this fairy tale as a child's dream of the adult world – or rather, a child's nightmare of it, since these children perceive the adults around them as deprived of the capacity to dream, and hence envious of their children's free and easy inhabitation of the landscape and logic of dreams, envious enough to wish to invade it themselves, an invasion which of course transforms their dreams into nightmares from which they cannot escape. And these are the generic terms we need to understand Jeunet's hybrid clone of the alien universe, his transfiguration of its fundamentally realistic terms into others equally capable of tapping the power of the medium of cinema as such; *Alien Resurrection* exhibits the appearance and logic of dreams and fairy tale rather than of the real world (even the world of the future, the reality of science fiction). The world viewed in this film is one in which the central protagonists are children in all but name, human beings inhabiting a world seen as if from the perspective of a child – hence one which invites them (and us) to accept the (physical and spiritual) absurdities and monstrosities of adults as normal, and to regard their (and our) instinctive sense of what is normal (whether in ourselves or in others) as monstrously or absurdly misaligned.

MONSTROUS CHILDREN

Even within the generally juvenile band of pirates trying to return to the *Betty*, two characters stand out as essentially childlike. Call's diminutive size implicitly suggests that this is her status, as does her fundamental spiritual innocence. She has involved herself in this potentially lethal farce purely to save the human race from itself – a race that, after creating the technology that created her (she is a robot built by robots), then chose to recall her (along with all her brothers and sisters) for immediate destruction; and her behaviour throughout the narrative is essentially compassionate. The film wavers between thinking of her virtue as a function of her programming, and as an aspect of her transcendence of it (for example, she has to be persuaded to interface with 'Father' to block Wren's progress to the *Betty*); but either way, as a new creation or offspring of the human, she incarnates the idea of childhood innocence. It is as if, from the child's perspective Jeunet invites us to inhabit, monstrosity and selfishness appear as a perversion of initial or original virtue by experience and culture, something we grow into as we grow up and hence something that might be avoided by avoiding the process of growing up; and by making his film's purest expression of that innocence a creature of synthetic circuitry rather than flesh and blood, Jeunet further associates the perversion of innocence with our fatedness to the body and its consequences – as if sexual maturation and spiritual purity appear mutually exclusive from the perspective of childhood.

However, the true child in this group is Ripley's clone. The film's opening scenes rapidly depict her *in vitro* conception, her post-operative emergence from a translucent caul or cocoon (as if the scientists' caesarian delivery of the alien queen from Ripley's clone was simultaneously her delivery from the queen, a transfiguring reconception or recreation of the human), and her schooling in human discourse and behaviour (the flashcard-and-stun-gun methods of her teachers subverting their implicit claim to be inducting her into, giving her a voice in, a genuinely civilized human form of life); in other words, we see her birth and her primary education – as if by the time of the *Betty*'s arrival, she is no more than a child in an adult's body. Hence, insofar as our access to the alien universe always flows through our identification with Ripley's perspective upon it, our point of view in this film is that of a newborn posthuman being – one to whom everything is new, and to whom the human perspective is no more natural than that of the aliens. In her case, then, to any child's natural oscillation between seeing the normal as absurd and the absurd as normal must be added a sense of species dislocation – the loss of any underlying sense of kinship with the alternately monstrous and risible grown-ups of her world (whether human or alien). Ripley's clone is not just seeing the world for the first time; she is seeing it as no one has ever seen it before (inhabiting it as much through smell as through vision, as much collectively as individually, as a mortal who has already died). Little wonder, then, that the alien universe as she experiences it should appear skewed or off-key, an uncanny parody or caricature of the one we have come to know over the years through the adult human eyes of her original.

Jeunet declares his sense that his dream or fantasy of that universe nevertheless remains faithful to its fundamental texture by making the first spoken words of his film (which precede our first view of Ripley's clone) a recitation by Sigourney Weaver of words first spoken by Newt in *Aliens*: 'My mummy always said that there were no monsters, no real ones – but there are'. This immediately declares that Weaver will here be occupying the perspective of a child; and it implies that what she sees will be the realization of a child's nightmare vision of the world. Jeunet thereby extends an idea developed in each of the preceding films, according to which the alien species is internally related to the human world of dreams – in *Alien*, the *Nostromo*'s crew wake from hypersleep into a nightmare; in *Aliens*, the monster's return is prefigured by its eruption into Ripley's dreams, and its ejection allows mother and child both to dream peacefully once again; in *Alien*[3], her enemy overcomes her resistance in her sleep. Against this background, Jeunet's presentation of the alien universe itself as having the texture of a child's nightmare appears as no more than a natural progression. But by identifying Ripley's clone as the child whose nightmare this world is, Jeunet further implies that the underlying logic of that universe can be traced to something childlike or childish in Ripley herself. More precisely, Jeunet appears to be suggesting that the vision of human fertility and sexuality which the alien species embodies is best understood as embodying the fantasies and fears of a child, and hence as expressive of a refusal or unwillingness to grow up.

But, however unwilling she may be, Ripley's clone is nevertheless required – by her accelerated biological development as much as by events on the *Auriga* – to grow up. Hence, the initial scenes of her childhood are quickly followed by her access to adolescence. Her gleeful delight in besting the *Betty's* crew on the basketball court, her nonchalant piercing of her own flesh, the bravado of her execution of the alien who killed Elgyn – accompanied throughout by her mastery of the mallrat dialogue that scriptwriter Joss Whedon first honed on *Buffy the Vampire Slayer* – all have that air of self-certainty, that uncomplicated pleasure in one's unfolding physical and intellectual powers, so familiar from adolescence. But the clone's sense of potency is irregularly punctured in an equally familiar way, first when she is forced by Call during their first meeting to admit to an underlying uncertainty about her own identity, and then more brutally when the group's travels confront her with the reality of her own fleshly origins.

When she discovers the room marked '1–7', she cannot avoid the chance to understand the number '8' tattooed on her arm – to understand, as in all children's tales, the riddle of her own identity. Behind the door she finds the results of the scientists' previous cloning attempts – seven hideously distorted forms, whose rapid progression through various misbegotten assemblages of gills, teeth and tails to a recognizably human and conscious, but scarred and tortured, number 7 indicate the eighth clone's kinship with the aliens, and the terrifying contingency of her own physical perfection. Beyond their manifestation of the monstrousness of the scientific project which produced her, these specimens function as a representation of the development of what is at once a new species and a new individual (as if declaring that, for Ripley's clone at least, ontogeny recapitulates phylogeny): they display nature's need to engender monstrosities if new species are to evolve, and the monstrous plasticity of any individual organism in its pre-birth development in the womb (or the test tube). Ripley's clone thus confronts the multiple, interlinked conditions of her own existence – as the meat by-product of a cloning process, as the sole member of a new species, and as a specific, individual creature.

Jeunet declares this scene's affinity with the confrontation in *Aliens* between Ripley and the alien queen in her nursery by arming Ripley's clone with a flamethrower, with which she proceeds to destroy the room and its contents. In part, of course, she is responding to the seventh clone's agonized desire for oblivion; but in widening her field of fire to embrace the whole room, Ripley's clone stirs our memory of her original's betrayal of her agreement with the alien queen when, in an excess of disgust at the latter's embodiment of fecundity, she attempts to torch the whole nursery. Jeunet thereby suggests that, for his posthuman protagonist, this destruction does far more than express her outrage at the cloning project. It also declares her anguish at the fact that the project gave her life by the merest accident, as if she is driven to deny not only the wickedness of which she is the offspring, but also the sheer arbitrariness of her own existence – its non-necessity, its dependence upon brute chance. And the conflagration further expresses her revulsion against the reality of her own origination in flesh and blood, against the body's unnerving capacity to mutate, its ineliminable vulnerability to violation and distortion, its unswerving drive to reshape itself from within (to develop from egg to adult) and its essential openness to being reshaped from without (to grafting, hybridity and evolution).

Ripley's clone thus finds herself incapable of doing what her original managed to do only at the moment, and in the manner of, her death – properly acknowledging what it might mean to be a creature of flesh and blood; she cannot see that, in responding so excessively to the seventh clone's request to 'Kill me', she gives expression to a desire to annihilate the conditions of her own existence – she cannot see that, in destroying these aborted or deformed versions of herself, she is in effect destroying herself (a perception incorporated in the scene itself by the fact that Sigourney Weaver plays the role of the seventh as well as the eighth clone, so that the flesh and blood human being who enacts this destruction is also the one who pleads for it).

But no such phantasms of self-destruction, however cathartic, can bring about the consummation they really desire; the transition from child to adult – the programmed transfiguration of the flesh into sexual maturity – is not to be avoided. Hence Ripley's clone is not permitted to reach the safety of the *Betty* without confronting the sexual potential of her already adult body, which means confronting the fact that the generativity of her flesh has always already been exploited – that she is, and has been from the first moment of her own independent existence, a mother: the mother of the monster.

In another of the film's more powerful sequences (a second trapdoor set into its parodic surface, through which we fall – with its protagonist – back into the deepest metaphysical dimensions of the alien universe), Ripley's clone is drawn down into the embrace of the alien species, luxuriating in her absorption into the writhing mass of its limbs and tails – as if engulfed by the very lability of organic being that she had earlier attempted to consume in fire (and that finds further expression elsewhere in the aliens' graceful adaptation to water, at once recalling their inhabitation of that medium when capturing Newt in *Aliens* and prefiguring their coming adaptation to the amniotic). But this reactivation of the alien aspect of her embodiment ends by delivering her (half-dazed, as if either still dreaming or just awakening from a dream – or perhaps in post-coital satiety, as if implying an orgasmic dimension to her experience of reincorporation into the alien community) to the alien queen's nursery, just in time to observe her offspring's delivery of another of her offspring. And in so doing, Ripley's clone perceives the initial activation of the human aspect of the alien queen's embodiment – her subjection to a reproductive cycle involving pregnancy, labour and birth.

Jeunet here succeeds in evoking a strong sense of tenderness towards the queen – compassion for the fact of her new, utterly alien, mode of victimization by her own body, for the fact that it results from her own gestation in the body of Ripley's clone (its being a sorrow bequeathed to her simply because she is the female offspring of a female, an aspect of her fleshly origin), and for the fact that (as a monstrous incarnation of male heterosexuality) its capacity to place all humans in the position of human females should ultimately result in its own occupation of that position.

In terms of the logic of the alien universe, however, it soon appears that Ripley's clone has not so much bequeathed a human mode of reproduction to her offspring as displaced it onto her. For the child who emerges from the queen's belly instinctively sees its true mother as monstrous, and turns instead to Ripley's clone; it is so horrified by the queen that it is prepared to kill her rather than acknowledge itself as her offspring – but it is prepared to see Ripley's clone as its mother, to see itself as flesh of that flesh. In other words, the alien queen gives birth to her mother's child; Ripley's clone attains motherhood without heterosexual intercourse, pregnancy or childbirth by sacrificing her true (but involuntarily conceived and delivered) daughter to what she thinks of as death-dealing invasions of her bodily integrity.

The clone is not entirely unresponsive to her (grand)child's sense of kinship with her; she finds herself capable of treating it with a certain tenderness, is reluctant to leave it, and hence incapable of an unqualified rejection of its assumption of her maternity. But the film's culminating course of events (as the *Betty* careers through Earth's atmosphere and away from the alien-infested *Auriga*) shows that she is equally incapable of an unqualified acceptance of it.

In part, this is motivated by the clone's reluctant but real concern for the humans on board the *Betty*, in part perhaps by vengeful grief over her (grand)child's role in the monstrous end of her true daughter. But most fundamentally, it flows from the fact that this child's sheer existence declares the generativity of her flesh and blood, and its form and nature declares its hybridity – its equal participation in human and alien nature. Hence the clone's acknowledgement of the child as hers would entail an acknowledgement of her own generativity and hybridity, of her own posthuman mode of being and its unavoidable drive towards reproduction and mutation. And Ripley's clone does not have it within her, despite her access to memories of her original's death, to make that acknowledgement.

Hence, she finds herself compelled not only to deny the child's plea for acknowledgement, but to destroy its source, and hence the possibility of its reiteration. As she soothes the child's fears and frustrations in the *Betty's* cargo bay, she uses her own acidic blood to incise a small hole in one of the windows, and the monstrous infant is gradually sucked through it, its pleading wails eventually silenced as the last particles of its body are squeezed out into space. This climax is an inflection of a familiar trope of the series: the first two films culminate with an alien's ejection into space through an airlock, the third with the alien queen's ejection from the universe as such. In *Alien Resurrection*, the alien child's end is a grotesque parody or inversion of its birth, and hence of birth as such: its recent emergence from an orifice in its unacknow-ledged mother's torso is recapitulated in reverse (hence negated or denied) by its being forced through a narrow opening to its death, by its undergoing a lethal expulsion from the technological carapace of its ideal mother's body. Ripley's clone watches the child's death with anguish and remorse; but this horrific destruction of her own flesh and blood is something she herself brings about, and she uses her own blood to do it – as if to deny with the very stuff of her own organic being the sole living proof of its generativity.

So when Ripley's clone stands on the threshold of a new, terrestrial life – a stranger about to enter the strange land that her original died to save from her alien kin – her diminutive companion is not the monstrous infant but Call, the childlike robot whose human inheritance is spiritual rather than fleshly, a paradigm of non-fecund embodiment (the sterile offspring of machines). This closing conjunction does not exactly suggest that the film's protagonist has overcome her original's psychic anxieties about her own embodiment; it rather confirms that Jeunet's inflection of the alien universe has only transposed its essential thematic coordinates – it has not transcended them.

But of course, the conjunction has another, more reflexive significance. For almost twenty years have passed in the life of the 'Alien' series, and as its unifying focus on the intimate otherness of Ripley and the alien has deepened and clarified, so has its dependence upon Sigourney Weaver. But twenty years is a long time in the life of a female star; in Weaver's case, it takes her well into her forties – a point at which it becomes increasingly difficult for many women actors (regardless of their mastery of their craft) to obtain substantial parts, and hence to maintain an audience and a career. It is easy to see *Alien Resurrection*'s casting of Winona Ryder in the role of Call as an attempt to graft a new female star onto the 'Alien' franchise, and thereby to break its dependence on Sigourney Weaver's continued attractiveness to cinema audiences; and it is also easy to see, amidst the psychic turbulence of the scene in room '1–7', something of Weaver's own anxieties about her status as a star – its dependence not only upon the fortunate interaction of her exact physiognomy with that of the movie camera, and with that of her monstrous other in this series, but also upon the continuation of that good fortune despite the inevitable physical transformations of ageing.

But the central truth of *Alien Resurrection* is surely that both kinds of anxiety are groundless. For Sigourney Weaver's performance is a marvel of economy, intelligence and physical fluidity; her subtle incarnation of genetic hybridity, her capacity to accommodate wild shifts of tone from sarcastic, adolescent one-liners to agonized psychic struggles, and her undeniably charismatic physical presence, hold together a film that is sometimes in danger of losing its grip on its audience, and together declare that she is at the peak of her powers. It seems plain that, if the series is allowed to continue in the terrestrial context that Jeunet holds open for his successor, it will do so only if Sigourney Weaver is prepared once again to submit herself to the vicissitudes of the camera (one might say, to its cloning or replication of her physical presence), and of the character whose life (and life after death) is now inextricably linked with her own cinematic identity.

Notes

INTRODUCTION

1 As will be evident, my main source of inspiration is the work of Stanley Cavell, whose books on film include *The World Viewed* (Harvard University Press: Cambridge, Mass., 1979), *Pursuits of Happiness* (Harvard University Press: Cambridge, Mass., 1981) and *Contesting Tears* (University of Chicago Press: Chicago, 1996) but whose philosophical reach extends much further. More occasional sources include Nietzsche, Heidegger and Wittgenstein.

ONE   KANE'S SON, CAIN'S DAUGHTER:
RIDLEY SCOTT'S *ALIEN* ONE

1 Barbara Creed, in '*Alien* and the Monstrous-feminine' (A. Kuhn [ed], *Alien Zone* [Verso: London, 1990), notes this aspect of the prologue; but her argument works through certain ideas of Julia Kristeva that are not, on my reading of the film, essential to grasping its logic; hence our accounts rapidly diverge.

2 cf. *The Claim of Reason* (Oxford University Press: Oxford, 1979), pp. 418–9.

3 In an out-take from the finished version of the film (included in the *Alien Trilogy* box set), Ripley is shown questioning Lambert about the sexuality of other crew-members – suggesting that Lambert's more conventionally feminine appearance is associated with a degree of promiscuity.

4 We never see J.F. Sebastian's execution or his corpse; Tyrell is murdered in a context in which, as we shall see, his human status is in doubt; and the violence directed at Deckard – whose human status has also been doubted – will be shown to have an educative function.

5 Stanley Cavell gives a detailed treatment of the logic of acknowledgement in the fourth part of *The Claim of Reason*.

6 This is a version of Stanley Cavell's characterization, in *The World Viewed* (Harvard University Press: Cambridge Mass., 1971).

TWO MAKING BABIES: JAMES CAMERON'S *ALIENS*

1 See chapters two and three of *The World Viewed*.
2 See his interview, released with the *Alien Trilogy* box set.
3 Scott in fact filmed a scene for *Alien* in which Ripley encountered a cocooned Dallas, but discarded it for reasons of pacing – cf. his interview released with the *Alien Trilogy* box set.
4 A conjunction exemplified in a scene restored in the Director's Cut, where – in its opening sweep of the *Sulaco* – the camera pans across an open locker door decorated with pornographic photographs to an equally pornographic array of pulse rifles.
5 The Director's Cut includes an early scene in which the fifty-seven years of Ripley's hypersleep are shown to have included the death of her only daughter, to whom she promised to return to in time for her birthday. The initial exclusion of this scene preserved *Aliens'* careful consistency with Ripley's nightmare vision of self and world, as declared in *Alien*; its subsequent incorporation sacrifices that consistency without modifying the counter-fleshly purity of the new family Cameron conceives of as Ripley's proper reward. It is a textbook example of the ways in which supposedly non-aesthetic considerations (the need to trim a movie to maximize potential daily box office) can engender aesthetic achievements, and of a director's ability to lose touch with his own best insights.
6 See chapter four of *The World Viewed*.
7 A claim recorded in 'The Making of *Terminator 2*'.

THREE MOURNING SICKNESS: DAVID FINCHER'S *ALIEN³*

1 As Richard Dyer notes in his useful discussion of this film, *Seven* (BFI Publishing: London, 1999).

FOUR   THE MONSTER'S MOTHER: JEAN-PIERRE JEUNET'S *ALIEN RESURRECTION*

1   It drives David Thomson to rewrite the script of *Alien Resurrection* altogether, rather than take it seriously as it stands – cf. his *The Alien Quartet* (Bloomsbury: London, 1998).